Essential Histories

The English Civil Wars
1642–1651

Peter Gaunt

First published in Great Britain in 2003 by Osprey Publishing,
Midland House, West Way, Botley, Oxford OX2 0PH, UK
44-02 23rd St, Suite 219, Long Island City, NY 11101, USA
Email: info@ospreypublishing.com

Transferred to digital print on demand 2009

First published 2003
Seventh impression 2008

Printed and bound by PrintOnDemand-Worldwide.com, Peterborough, UK

A CIP catalogue record for this book is available from the British Library

ISBN: 978 1 84176 417 7

Editorial by Sally Rawlings
Page layout by Ken Vail Graphic Design, Cambridge, UK
Cartography by The Map Studio
Typeset in Monotype Gill Sans and ITC Stone Serif
Index by David Worthington
Picture research by Image Select International
Originated by PPS Grasmere, Leeds, UK

FOR A CATALOGUE OF ALL BOOKS PUBLISHED BY OSPREY
MILITARY AND AVIATION PLEASE CONTACT:

Osprey Direct, c/o Random House Distribution Center,
400 Hahn Road, Westminster, MD 21157
Email: uscustomerservice@ospreypublishing.com

Osprey Direct, The Book Service Ltd, Distribution Centre,
Colchester Road, Frating Green, Colchester, Essex, CO7 7DW
Email: customerservice@ospreypublishing.com

www.ospreypublishing.com

Contents

Introduction

On the day after he had led one wing of the parliamentary army to victory in one of the largest, probably the bloodiest and in many ways the most important and decisive battle of the English civil wars, Oliver Cromwell wrote to his brother-in-law, Valentine Walton. Justifiably famous and unquestionably moving, Cromwell's letter conveyed both good news and bad: 'It's our duty to sympathise in all mercies; that we may praise the Lord together in chastisements or trials, that so we may sorrow together.' In euphoric and breathless phrases, Cromwell recounted the 'great victory given unto us, such as the like never was since this war began'. The battle appeared 'an absolute victory'. 'We never charged but we routed the enemy ... God made them as stubble to our swords ... of twenty-thousand the Prince hath not four-thousand left.' But Cromwell also had to break the news to Walton that his son had perished on the battlefield: 'God hath taken away your eldest son by a cannon-shot. It brake his leg. We were necessitated to have it cut off, whereof he died.' Throughout the letter, Cromwell's deep religious faith was clear, in his unswerving belief that the military victory was due to God's support for His cause – 'a great favour from the Lord', 'Give glory, all the glory, to God' – and in his assurances that Walton's son, 'a precious young man, fit for God', had shared this faith and had drawn comfort from it as he lay dying. 'You have cause to bless the Lord,' he told Walton, for 'there is your precious child full of glory, to know sin nor sorrow any more', 'a glorious saint in Heaven'.

Cromwell's letter highlights many aspects of the English civil wars – their scale, involving tens of thousands of combatants; the extent of the suffering, with large

'Cromwell after the battle of Marston Moor', by Ernest Crofts. Crofts was one of several Victorian artists who specialised in civil war scenes, a very popular genre during the 19th century, though the images often owe more to a romantic and dramatic licence than to strict historical accuracy. (Bridgeman Art Library)

numbers dead, dying or injured; the horrors
and brutality, with the unsuccessful
battlefield amputation and the attempt to
console a father who had lost his eldest son
in action; and a glimpse of the deep
convictions, matters of faith or principle,
that drove so many forward into and
through a brutal civil war, and which led
them to take up arms and to kill and maim
fellow countrymen, in many cases
neighbours, friends and relations. These are
now the predominant images of the civil
wars. Earlier generations of historians
sometimes played down their nature,
arguing that the bulk of the population were
little affected by them, portraying the
conflict as limited and dignified, a civilised
and almost genteel affair, and emphasising
the elements of lordly disdain and aversion
to the war found, for example, in Sir William
Waller's oft-quoted letter to Sir Ralph Hopton
of summer 1643, with its description of 'this
war without an enemy' and its hope that
they should both 'in a way of honour, and
without personal animosities' act out 'those
parts that are assigned us in this tragedy'.

Recent work has demonstrated that the
English civil wars were nothing like this. A
large proportion of the population was
directly involved in the fighting: during each
of the campaigning seasons of 1643, 1644
and 1645 it is estimated that more than one
in 10 of the male population aged between
16 and 60 was in arms and that during the
civil wars as a whole perhaps one in four of
the adult male population of England and
Wales took up arms at some stage. Many
more civilians were caught up in the
conflict, in the 150 or so towns that suffered
attack or substantial war-related damage, in
the enforced billeting, plundering, violence
and disease which a civil war army on the
move brought with it, and in meeting the
very heavy, repeated and quite
unprecedented financial and material
demands imposed by both sides to sustain
their war efforts. In the course of the war,
especially as the tide turned in parliament's
favour, many royalists, neutrals and
Catholics were deprived of some or all of

their property. Fatalities in the hundreds of
battles, skirmishes and raids that took place
in England and Wales, together with the
increased mortality through the spread of
disease, caused something approaching
200,000 deaths – an overall death-rate in
terms of the proportion of the population
slightly higher than that suffered in the First
World War and significantly higher than that
in the Second. Landscapes of all sorts were
destroyed, overthrown or remodelled – not
only the physical landscape, with
destruction to towns and villages, castles,
churches and manor houses, but also other
landmarks which had shaped people's lives,
as the fundamentals of central government
and local administration, of church, religion
and faith, of justice and the peaceful
possession of property, of society, ideas and
culture, were overthrown, profoundly shaken
or substantially remoulded. The English civil
wars were bloody, brutal and at times
barbaric, and although in some ways they
proved to be a catalyst for change and
innovation, they also caused death,
destruction and deprivation on a huge scale.

This study concentrates on the civil wars in
England and Wales, particularly the main civil
war fought from summer 1642 until summer
1646, though the later conflicts of 1648 and
1651 are briefly examined in the closing
chapters. Scottish and Irish developments are
covered only where they directly impinged on
the conflict in England and Wales. This
account is primarily military, though other
issues and developments are sketched in to
provide a more rounded context. It explores
the roles, actions and experiences of the elites
who directed the wars but also, where sources
permit, of some of the ordinary people,
soldiers and civilians, who participated or
were caught up in the conflict. We should
never forget that we are dealing with real
people, individuals with their own hopes and
fears, pleasures and pains, every bit as alive
and animated as ourselves, whose lives were
often changed, improved, cruelly shattered or
violently ended by the civil wars.

As an old man writing in the first decade
of the 18th century Richard Gough had a

clear recollection of the conflict as it affected his home parish of Myddle in northern Shropshire. He recalled as a schoolboy being taken into the church when a royalist raiding party from Shrawardine Castle ran into some parliamentarians from Moreton Corbet. The royalist commander, Cornet Collins, was shot 'through the body with a carbine shot' outside the village smithy and was carried into the smith's house. The following day young Gough accompanied the vicar, who prayed with the dying royalist, and 60 years later he still recalled the sight of 'the cornet lying on the bed, and much blood running along the floor'. Richard Gough's experience of the English civil wars, though very limited, was dramatic and vivid, and the blood-red image of a

Moreton Corbet Castle in Shropshire housed a small royalist garrison for much of the war. On the far left is the ruin of the medieval castle, in the centre the gutted shell of a domestic range added during the reign of Elizabeth I. (Author's collection)

dying soldier stayed with him into old age; he never forgot his civil war. Gough was just one of over five million English and Welsh men, women and children who, directly or indirectly, willingly or unwillingly, were caught up in the unprecedented conflict of the mid-17th century and whose lives and emotions were touched by it. For all but a few, their stories died with them and are now lost to us, but doubtless each would have had a unique tale to tell of their own experience of the English civil wars.

England and Wales 1642–51

England and Wales at the time of the civil wars, showing sites and locations mentioned in the text.

Chronology

1603 James VI of Scotland becomes James I of England
1625 Death of James I; accession of Charles I
1625–29 Rule with parliaments in England War with Spain and France
1629–40 Rule without parliaments in England – The Personal Rule
1631 Sir Thomas Wentworth, later Earl of Strafford, appointed to govern Ireland
1633 William Laud appointed Archbishop of Canterbury
1636 New canons for Scotland
1637 New prayer book for Scotland
1638 Scottish National Covenant
1638–40 Political and ecclesiastical revolution in Scotland
1639 **May–June** First Scots' or Bishops' War
1640 **April–May** Short Parliament
August–October Second Scots' or Bishops' War
November Long Parliament meets
1640–41 Personnel and policies of the Personal Rule removed
1641 **October** Irish Catholic rebellion begins
1642 **January** King's attempted arrest of the Five Members
April King denied entry into Hull
August Skirmish at Marshall's Elm Parliamentary operation against Portsmouth
King raises standard at Nottingham
September Parliamentary army at Northampton, then Worcester
King's army at Shrewsbury
Skirmish at Powick Bridge
October Battle of Edgehill
November Royalists storm Brentford
Stand-off at Turnham Green
King falls back to Oxford
1643 **January** Battle of Boconnoc/Braddock Down

March Battle of Hopton Heath
Skirmish at Highnam
Battle of Seacroft Moor
April Skirmish on Ancaster Heath
Battle of Ripple
Royalists take Lichfield
Parliamentarians take Hereford
Skirmish on Sourton Down
Parliamentarians take Reading
May Parliamentarians take Grantham
Skirmish at Belton
Battle of Stratton
June Skirmish at Chalgrove
Battle of Adwalton Moor
July Battle of Lansdown Hill
Battle of Roundway Down
Parliamentarians take Gainsborough
Royalists take Bristol
Battle of Gainsborough
August–September Siege of Gloucester
September First Battle of Newbury
Parliament abandons Reading
September–October Blockade and siege of Hull
October Battle of Winceby
November Parliamentary invasion of north-east Wales rebuffed
December Royalist invasion of Sussex rebuffed
1644 **January** Scots enter England
Battle of Nantwich
March Royalists relieve Newark; parliamentary army surrenders
Battle of Cheriton
April–July Siege of York
May Royalists storm Stockport and Bolton
June Battle of Cropredy Bridge
July Royalists relieve York
Battle of Marston Moor
Parliamentarians take York
August Parliamentary army expelled from Lostwithiel

September Parliamentary army
surrenders near Fowey
Parliamentarians take Montgomery
Battle of Montgomery
October Second Battle of Newbury
Winter 1644–45 Self-Denying Ordinance
passed and New Model Army created
1645 **February** Parliamentarians take
Shrewsbury
May Royalists storm Leicester
June Battle of Naseby
July Battle of Langport
Parliamentarians take Bridgwater
August Skirmish on Colby Moor
September Parliamentarians take
Bristol
Battle of Rowton Moor
September–February 1646 Siege and
bombardment of Chester
October Parliamentarians take Basing
House
1646 **January** Skirmish at Bovey Tracey
February Parliamentarians take
Chester
Battle of Torrington
March Royalist army surrenders near

TruroSkirmish at Stow-in-the-Wold
May King surrenders to the Scots
outside Newark
Parliamentarians take Newark
June Parliamentarians take Oxford
1646–47 Failure to reach a firm
settlement; growing divisions
1648 **March** Rising against parliament
in Pembrokeshire
May Royalist rebellion in Kent
Battle of St Fagans
Parliamentary fleet mutinies
May–July Siege of Pembroke
June Battle of Maidstone
June–August Siege of Colchester
August Battle of Preston
Pursuit of Scottish-royalist army
through south Lancashire
December Long Parliament
purged
1649 **January** Trial and execution of the
king
February Monarchy and House of
Lords abolished
May Republic or 'Commonwealth'
established

The causes and origins of the English civil wars

The debate on the causes and origins of the English civil wars is intense and unresolved. Since the emergence in the 19th century of scholarly, source-based interpretations, very different theories have been advanced. At times, something approaching consensus has been achieved, but discordant voices have always challenged the then orthodoxy and produced contrasting theories, and in due course the consensus has collapsed. At other times, no single line has carried much weight and a range of differing interpretations have been given currency. In the early 21st century we are going through a period of discordance, with no single interpretation which most historians either hold to or are reacting against. Instead, the field appears rather cluttered.

It is hardly surprising that later generations of historians have struggled to locate the origins of the wars, for many contemporaries were unsure or divided about their causes. The parliamentarian Bulstrode Whitelocke, for one, professed himself baffled, writing of the position in summer 1642, 'it is strange to note how we have insensibly slid into the beginning of a civil war by one unexpected accident after another, as waves of the sea which have brought us thus far and we scarce know how'. But other contemporaries attempted a more sophisticated analysis and claimed to detect a pattern. The royalist Edward Hyde, later Earl of Clarendon, believed that war resulted from a series of blunders made by both sides in the years before 1642 in their handling of problems in central government and administration. In other words, he pointed to a war whose causes were short-term and in essence political and constitutional (including the handling of religion and the state church). On the other hand, James Harrington believed that the war sprang from changes in society and the economy which he traced back to the reign of the first Tudor, Henry VII, and to developing tensions between the old landed elite and a newer, rising middle group. In other words, he pointed to a war whose causes were long-term and in essence socio-economic. These key variables – long-term or short-term, political and constitutional (including religion and the church) or socio-economic – provide a matrix into which most subsequent interpretations can be placed.

During the 19th and early 20th centuries the emphasis was upon long-term political, constitutional and religious causation, with the so-called Whig historians focusing on a political and constitutional power-struggle between crown and parliament, particularly the House of Commons, underway by the reigns of Henry VIII and Elizabeth I, compounded by disagreements between a conservative crown supported by the religious elite and a group of radical, reform-minded puritans over the future of the state church. For the Whigs, the civil wars of the 1640s, as much a Puritan Revolution as a political and constitutional contest, were the culmination of a century or more of secular and religious conflict. During the middle decades of the 20th century many historians, Marxists and others, argued that the civil wars resulted from long-term socio-economic change and were the consequence of growing tension between a declining feudal order dominated by the old aristocracy and a new, emerging, innovative, capitalist class of gentry and urban and rural middle classes. For Marxist historians, these changes in the socio-economic balance of power, which could be traced back to the early Tudor period, if not before, resulted in a bourgeois revolution of the mid-17th century. During the 1970s and 1980s the field was dominated

Bulstrode Whitelocke claimed that the descent into war in 1642 was the result not of a logical sequence of events or of any deep-seated and long-term causes, but rather of a succession of unexpected accidents, writing gloomily of the imminent conflict, 'what the issue of it will be no man alive can tell. Probably few of us now here may live to see the end of it.' (Ann Ronan Picture Library)

A contemporary or near-contemporary portrait panel of
James I, the first Stuart king of England, from a window of
Corpus Christi church, Tremeirchion, North Wales.
(Author's collection)

by revisionist historians, who returned to political, constitutional and religious causation but who emphasised short-term explanations. Most revisionists argued that the early Stuart state was strong and united, with evidence of harmony, co-operation and consensus, and that civil war resulted from problems in the running of church and state which emerged predominately after the accession of Charles I in 1625, many of them stemming from Charles' own personal, political and religious approach to government. During the closing decades of the 20th century many historians sought rather deeper, longer-term causes of the war, some within England and Wales – including the weakness of royal finances and religious division over whether the Church of England needed further reformation – others found further afield. In particular, during the 1980s and 1990s many historians stressed that the English civil wars had been preceded and shaped by failed wars against Scotland and rebellion in Ireland and argued that all these conflicts stemmed from one or more common causes, a British problem or problems. They suggested that when, in 1625, the British multiple kingdom passed to a monarch who was careless of the rights and distinctiveness of his component territories and who tactlessly sought to impose change and greater religious conformity, Charles created crisis, collapse and war throughout his three kingdoms.

Although all these 'top-down' interpretations attracted considerable support for a time, none has proved durable and each in turn has produced a growing tide of criticism and scepticism. Meanwhile, over the past few decades some historians have explored divisions at the local level in the period before and during the civil wars. Taking a 'bottom-up' approach, these historians analyse how and why the nation as a whole, or particular parts of it, divided in the early 1640s, and seek to explore the views and outlooks not only of the provincial elites but also of the ordinary mass of the population. They have often found that the provincial population took an active and well-informed interest in developments at the centre, that ordinary people held strong views about developments in church and state, which overlay provincial and local concerns. Many historians have gone on to suggest that the secular and religious policies pursued at the centre in the pre-war decades created or exacerbated fractures in provincial society and that these not only help explain how the people of England and Wales divided once war began but also formed an essential element in causing the civil wars. Deep and wide divisions in English and Welsh society – for some historians principally over religion, for others involving a wider mixture of social, economic and cultural factors too – mirrored the divisions at the centre, and this explains why the towns and countryside of England and Wales divided into civil war so quickly and readily after elite relations at the centre had broken down.

In short, historians remain divided on the causes of the English civil wars. Some focus on local and provincial society and argue that divisions amongst the masses are crucial in explaining the outbreak of war, for no matter how and why the political or social elites may have fallen out, full-scale civil war occurred only because of much broader and deeper fractures within English and Welsh society. Others see this as a secondary issue, helping to explain the spread of war and the pattern of loyalties once it began, but arguing that the war was actually caused by divisions within the elites. A few historians continue to focus on socio-economic elites, on changes in the fortunes of, and tensions between, the old aristocracy and the landed gentry or middle classes. Many more focus on problems in the running of church and state, on a range of long-, medium- and short-term difficulties in the political, constitutional and religious structure and administration of England and Wales. These often include the strains caused by an outdated system of state finance which by the 17th century left the crown struggling to run the country in peacetime and in dire straits in times of emergency or war (whose

A portrait panel of Charles I, again from a window of Corpus Christi church, Tremeirchion. While most civil wars in England had been fought between rival claimants to the throne for possession of the crown, the civil wars of the mid-17th century were exceptional, for no-one seriously doubted that Charles was the rightful king. What was at stake during the 1640s was how Charles should rule, the policies he should pursue and the powers he should exercise, not whether he was the true king. (Author's collection)

costs and complexities were escalating); unease with and within the state church about its future direction and the desirability and course of further reformation; and evidence of growing political dislocation amongst the elite, with conflict between crown and parliament, disagreement over key policies and perhaps also over matters of broader principle, ideology or political philosophy. Historians who point to these sorts of tensions often emphasise that their origins lay in the Tudor or early Stuart period, but that they deteriorated markedly after Charles I came to the throne in 1625. They tend to emphasise the shortcomings and failings of the new king who, by mishandling a difficult inheritance and through his own personality and policies, turned potential problems into real ones, needlessly kicking awake dogs which had slumbered under James I. In this interpretation, Charles I was not the only cause of the civil wars, for their origins lay far deeper and pre-dated his accession, often by many decades. But his mishandling of the situation contributed greatly to the crises and confrontations which during the 1640s dragged England and Wales down into civil war.

Charles I and the descent into war in three kingdoms, 1625–42

Charles I was a hard-working monarch with sincere convictions. However, some contemporaries and many historians have viewed him as a cold, formal, unattractive figure, unable or unwilling to explain himself, convince doubters or win affection, a man temperamentally and perhaps intellectually unsuited to holding power at a time of so many potential difficulties. From the outset, Charles pursued divisive and sometimes unworkable policies, refused to conciliate or compromise in the face of difficulties and instead pressed ahead in the belief that a combination of his own iron will, a widely-shared respect for monarchy, divine support, duplicity and if need be physical force would drive through his chosen policies and ensure obedience. Although his kingdoms appeared to remain internally at peace and orderly until the late 1630s, most historians believe that Charles' approach and policies were provoking a rising tide of tension and dislocation. This may explain not only why the king's position collapsed so rapidly in all his kingdoms in 1638–42 but also why instability in one kingdom quickly destabilised its neighbours.

By the late 1630s Charles had aroused considerable opposition in England and Wales. In the latter half of the 1620s he went to war against France and Spain, mounting expensive, badly-organised and poorly-led campaigns which were disastrous failures.

The royal arms from the façade of the King's Manor in York. In the pre-war years this was the seat of the king's Council of the North and a residence of Sir Thomas Wentworth. (Author's collection)

Between 1625 and 1629 he conferred with three parliaments, each of which criticised his war policy and proved very slow at voting money. To cover his spiralling debts, Charles imposed exactions without parliamentary consent. The king's religious policies also caused problems, for he favoured high church, ceremonial Anglicanism, called 'Arminianism' or 'Laudianism', after William Laud, the king's closest religious adviser and, from 1633, Archbishop of Canterbury. It was opposed not only by godly reformers but also by many moderate believers who viewed Charles' innovations as undesirable and smelling of Catholicism. In the face of growing parliamentary criticism, the king determined to rule for a time without further parliaments in England and Wales and called none between 1629 and 1640.

During this period of Personal Rule, Charles directly oversaw government, employing his prerogative and executive powers to the full. Expenditure was curbed, not least by making and maintaining peace overseas, while income was boosted by exploiting existing sources and by reviving a range of feudal dues, so that for much of the 1630s the regime was financially strong. At the same time, Charles and Laud were able to push ahead with their religious policies, imposing more rigid, ritualistic and ceremonial forms of worship, physically beautifying and rearranging churches. Direct opposition was muted, for in the face of occasional legal challenges, the courts consistently found in the king's favour, and they were prone to punish harshly the few outspoken critics of royal policy. On the surface at least, the Personal Rule in England and Wales appeared to be running smoothly.

As king of Scotland, Charles was largely ignorant of, and unknown to, his subjects north of the border. In the 1630s he attempted to change religion in Scotland and to bring its church closer to the Church of England by imposing new canons and a prayer book modelled on English versions. This crystallised Scottish discontent, for they symbolised the approach of a distant and authoritarian crown careless of Scottish rights, the Anglicisation of Scotland and its government and the Anglicanisation of Scotland and its church. Most Scots viewed their Presbyterian church as purer and more reformed than the Church of England, and there was strong and widespread resistance to attempts to undo the Scottish reformation. The king lost control of the situation and the government and administration of Scotland passed to his opponents, the Covenanters, who in 1638–40 effected a revolution in church and state, leaving the king little power north of the border. Charles sought to re-establish royal control over Scotland by resorting to arms, seeking to use the military resources of his other kingdoms to crush the Scots. Charles fought two Scots' or Bishops' Wars, in summer 1639 and 1640. The first ended with an inconclusive truce, but the second resulted in a decisive Scottish victory and the occupation of the far northern counties of England by the Scottish army.

In April 1640 Charles had met an English parliament, thus ending his Personal Rule, and sought support and money to enable him to renew war against Scotland. Instead, that parliament proved overwhelmingly critical, seeking redress of grievances, and Charles dissolved this Short Parliament after barely three weeks and without a penny voted. However, having fought and lost another war against the Scots in summer 1640, Charles was in a very different position when he summoned and met another English parliament that autumn. He had been roundly defeated militarily, part of England was occupied by a hostile army demanding further payment, his two disastrous wars had left him saddled with huge debts and all-but bankrupt, his subjects in England and Wales had seized the opportunity presented by the king's difficulties to stop paying their taxes and above all Charles had been humiliated and left with little room for manoeuvre. When what became known as the Long Parliament began work in November, it held the whip hand and it knew it. Charles, too, recognised that for the moment he would have to give ground and make concessions to a parliament he could neither ignore nor dissolve at will.

The mistakes and divisions of the late 1620s, the personnel and policies of the Personal Rule, the disastrous wars against fellow-Protestants in Scotland, the dubious financial and religious innovations, all stuck in the craw of the vast majority of MPs and peers as they got to work in the closing weeks of 1640. During its opening year, a united parliament swept away much of the personnel and policies of the Personal Rule. Laud was imprisoned, the king's chief secular adviser, Sir Thomas Wentworth, Earl of Strafford, was condemned and executed, other royal ministers fled abroad, most of the feudal dues revived in the 1630s were abolished, it was firmly established that new taxes required parliamentary consent and some of the post-1625 religious innovations were reversed, though the king's critics trod more carefully here, aware of the divisive potential of religious reform. At the same time, the position of parliament itself was made more secure by legislation ensuring that the Long Parliament could not be dissolved except with its own consent and that henceforth no more than three years could elapse between two successive parliaments.

Civil war was not possible in England and Wales in 1640–41, for the king was facing a tide of opposition inside and outside parliament, and lacked a substantial body of support willing to fight for him. Instead, the crisis was apparently being resolved peacefully, within parliament. By the spring and summer of 1642 the position was very different. The political elite had split asunder, the king had gained a party at the centre and was rapidly gaining one in the provinces, and two different, distant and physically separated groups were preparing to go to war. What had occurred in the interim to account for these dramatic changes?

Part of the answer is to be found in Ireland, which had been governed by Sir Thomas Wentworth for most of the 1630s. His brutal rule alienated most groups there,

including the majority Catholic population as well as some of the minority Protestant community who were deprived of their estates. Wentworth's recall to England in 1640 and his fall and execution in 1641 left an enormous power vacuum in Ireland, as well as a legacy of discontent. The majority Catholic population, in particular, became nervous, worried by virulent anti-Catholic sentiments emanating from both the English parliament and the victorious Scottish Covenanters, some of whom were airing grand plans for a British-wide Protestant religious settlement. On the night of 22–23 October 1641, acting in co-ordination, many of the Irish Catholics of Ulster rose up in rebellion, and in the following days and weeks rebellion spread to the rest of Ireland. By the end of the winter most of Ireland was under the control of Catholic rebels. Greatly exaggerated atrocity tales soon began circulating in England and Scotland, horrifying the English parliament and raising the political temperature. The Catholic rebels claimed to be acting with the king's support and waved a royal commission, almost certainly forged. Although he acted swiftly to condemn the Irish Catholics, Charles fell under suspicion that he had colluded with them and fear of Catholic plots intensified. Above all, while everyone was agreed that an army would have to be raised in England and Wales and sent over to protect surviving Protestant communities, crush the rebellion and restore English rule, many doubted whether Charles could be trusted to command it. There were fears that he would deploy it not in Ireland against Catholic rebels but in England against parliament and its supporters.

Thus the Irish rebellion brought into stark relief one of several unresolved issues concerning the role and power of the monarchy and the future settlement, upon which Charles now took a stand. In terms of the military arm, Charles stood firm that the king was automatically commander-in-chief and that all military power rested with him alone. But many felt that he could not be trusted with an army and that alternative arrangements had to be made. In terms of the executive arm, Charles stood firm that the king had full and sole power to appoint, dismiss and direct officers of state and various executive bodies, notably the Privy Council. Again, many critics were demanding that parliament should have the right to make or vet such appointments. Perhaps even more thorny was the question of religion and the church. Although most members of the political elite were agreed in 1640–41 that the Church of England should be de-Arminianised and the post-1625 innovations removed, some wanted no more than a return to the church of Elizabeth I and James I; by autumn 1641 that was the line being taken by Charles. But others wanted to push much further, to complete the work left half finished in the 16th century, and radically to reform the Church of England, perhaps by abolishing episcopacy.

In autumn 1641 some of the political elite wanted to press ahead further to limit the military and political powers of the king and to create a purer church. They genuinely believed that additional changes were needed in order to avoid renewed clashes and another crisis. Many also feared that if the reform programme stalled, Charles would retain enough power to enable him in the future to reverse concessions which he had made insincerely and only under duress during

1640–41. But by autumn 1641 other members of the political elite believed that reform had gone far enough, that the abuses of the Personal Rule had now been corrected and that the king should and must be trusted. To push further was unnecessary and dangerous, and risked undermining the divinely appointed and anointed monarchy, destabilising the state and unleashing turmoil and heresy. In standing firm on remaining points of issue, Charles began consciously and effectively to portray himself as defending the traditional church and state, as a bulwark against parliamentary innovation and the anarchy it would unleash. It was a stance which struck a chord with many and brought tangible results. Parliamentary debates and votes during the autumn and winter of 1641–42 confirmed that the political elite was becoming increasingly fragmented, that support for further change was declining and that many former critics of royal policy were now moving to support the king.

The early 17th-century communion rail in St Mary's church, Chediston, Suffolk. One of the most contentious aspects of Charles' high church policy of the pre-war years was the introduction of permanent, east end altars which were railed off to prevent the laity approaching the altar. Only the clergy could enter this privileged area, emphasising their enhanced role as intermediaries between God and the congregation. (Author's collection)

During the winter and spring of 1641–42 there was growing division and distrust between this royalist group and the parliamentary reformers. The latter pressed ahead with their programme, drawing up a list of royal abuses, advancing legislation implying or asserting that the king no longer had sole military power, and eventually laying claim to full control over the armed forces and the executive. Some of these were genuine goals, but others are better seen as part of a phoney or paper war. For his part, the king generally reacted moderately, agreeing to some limited reforms but also refusing to give assent to many of parliament's demands, and sticking by his line that he represented and was defending the existing church, constitution and rule of law. However, at times Charles acted rashly, over-estimating his strength or panicked into unwise moves. Amidst scenes of growing public disorder in London, in early January 1642 he personally intervened in parliament in an unsuccessful attempt to arrest some of his leading critics, whom he accused of treason. Soon after, fearing for the personal safety of himself and his family, and aware that London's militia and the Tower of London were now in the hands of men loyal to parliament, he decided to quit the capital, heading first to Hampton Court, and then north, eventually setting up his court in York. From there, he and his advisers issued various declarations and rebuttals over the summer, engaging in the paper and propaganda war with parliament.

The physical separation of two substantial and increasingly hostile parties raised the possibility of civil war. But many historians suggest that war could only have begun if there were also deeper divisions within society, bodies of supporters within local communities who were prepared to fight. The thirst for news and information in the provinces had been whetted by the dramatic developments of the early 1640s and had in part been met by a huge expansion in printed material. Thus large sections of the population were probably well aware of the growing crisis in 1642 and had informed views about it. Despite widespread dismay at the drift towards war, with evidence of apathy, neutralism and a desire for peace, the call to arms met a sufficiently strong response to enable both sides to raise credible armies and begin a war.

As each side sought to raise an army in summer 1642, adopting very similar methods, there were inevitably a number of tense stand-offs or real and occasionally bloody fights, as rival recruiting agents worked in the same area or as one side sought to secure a stronghold then in the hands of the other. Thus in April the king and his forces were denied entry into Kingston upon Hull by its pro-parliamentary governor, in mid-July royalists attacked but failed to capture Manchester, whose townspeople were sympathetic to the parliamentary cause and were supported by some pro-parliamentary troops, and in early August parliamentary forces launched an operation to capture Portsmouth, then in royalist hands. Many other clashes are not so well documented and it is now impossible to say with certainty when and where the first fatality of the English civil wars occurred. A Mancunian weaver, perhaps called Richard Perceval, killed on 15 July in the defence of Manchester, is often pointed to as the first civil war casualty, but in reality we cannot be sure. There certainly were more fatalities in Somerset in early August, when a body of royalist horse and dragoons ambushed a much larger party of parliamentarians at Marshall's Elm, firing several volleys of shot and killing at least three outright and leaving a further 20 or so fatally wounded. 'And thus innocently began this cursed war', the royalist commander that day later recalled. Although other confrontations ensued in the following fortnight, the action at Marshall's Elm on 4 August may well have been the bloodiest confrontation of the summer to pre-date the formal outbreak of civil war. This occurred on 22 August when, in a theatrical and medieval gesture, Charles I raised his standard at Nottingham.

Raising the armies, 1642

Although there were men in arms in Ireland in 1642, England and Wales had no standing army and almost no troops in place as king and parliament set about raising armies in spring and summer 1642. Both sides might, however, look to recruit men from the existing militia units, the part-time self-defence forces found in all counties of England and Wales; some of the larger towns had their own separate militia units or trained bands. In theory, all able-bodied males between 16 and 60 were liable to serve and to muster several times a year for training. In practice, it was hard to compel attendance and the numbers serving in each county were modest, often under 2,000. Even so, it remained a numerically significant force, for on the eve of the civil wars it should have totalled around 100,000 men, about 95,000 foot and 5,000 horse. Although some units, such as those of Lancashire and the unusually well-trained and committed London trained bands, were formidable and had real military potential, many militia forces were amateurish and poor. One officer alleged that training generally comprised 'a little casual hurrying over their postures' before retiring to a nearby inn, first to salute their captain with 'a brave volley of shot' as he entered, and then rapidly to join him in alcoholic revelry. In any case, while men were happy to spend a few days a year playing at war and drinking, they often had no stomach for the real thing and no inclination in 1642 to volunteer. Moreover, by long tradition each militia was a self-defence force, designed to protect its own county, and many were unwilling to march away in a field army and campaign elsewhere. As war loomed, both sides sought to call out county militias, win them over and recruit from their ranks, but the response was patchy.

Instead, both sides soon launched fresh recruiting drives. Royalist and parliamentary county commissioners were appointed and empowered to raise troops in the counties where they held influence. Richard Gough described how one royalist commissioner operated. Sir Paul Harris sent out warrants notifying the inhabitants of the hundred that he would be holding an open air recruiting meeting on Myddle Hill, in north Shropshire, on a set date and requesting all male inhabitants between 16 and 60, whether heads of households, sons, servants or lodgers, to attend. Gough went along to watch 'this great show'. 'And there I saw a multitude of men, and upon the highest bank of the hill' he noted one of Harris' assistants 'standing, with a paper in his hand, and three or four soldiers' pikes, stuck upright in the ground by him; and there he made a proclamation, that if any person would serve the king, as a soldier in the wars, he should have fourteen groats a week for his pay'. The offer clearly struck a chord, for Gough estimated that at least 20 men from Myddle and two adjoining villages volunteered. With less success, Sir William Brereton and some fellow parliamentary commissioners attempted to recruit in Chester in early August, but they met with rowdy opposition, 'a great tumult'. The city authorities intervened and confiscated their drum, but Brereton and his colleagues 'continued the tumult' and were eventually escorted from the city under guard, in part to protect them from the abuse of the citizens.

By summer 1642 both the king and the parliamentary commander-in-chief were also commissioning as colonels of completely new regiments individual members of the elite, who would then go out and raise troops. For example, in August 1642 the king commissioned Lord Paget colonel of a new foot regiment. Paget returned to his native Staffordshire to recruit, contacting neighbouring landowners, seeking their support and in some cases appointing them or their sons captains within his fledgling regiment. These then launched a broader recruitment drive in and around Staffordshire, not only drawing upon pools of kinsmen, tenants, servants and other dependants but also going around beating the drum and seeking volunteers in the villages and countryside. Within a month, Paget and his local captains had raised around 1,000 men. The volunteers of summer 1642 probably came forward for a variety of reasons, encompassing the lure of adventure and excitement, the offer of regular pay and employment in which clothing, food and shelter would be provided by the employer, ties of kinship, friendship, tenancy or service, and a clear and principled commitment to fight for their chosen cause, a conscious and informed decision based upon political or religious beliefs. In these ways and from these sources, each side had succeeded in raising the equivalent of over 20 regiments by the

end of the summer, and by October each probably had over 20,000 men in arms, divided between a main field army and detached units.

Surviving sources reveal the identity of some of these early volunteers and give insight into why they volunteered. We should beware, however, for these accounts come from a small number of the more literate middle and upper social strata, and may not be typical of the thousands who joined up in 1642. Many early participants on both sides wrote that they felt compelled to fight in response to the actions of the other party and in defence of themselves, their families, their rights and liberties. For example, the royalist William Chillingworth said that he and his colleagues joined up to 'defend our lives and livelihood, wives, children, houses and lands', while the parliamentarian Richard Hubberthorn claimed to be fighting 'in a defensive way for our rights and liberties'. Many stressed that they had not made a sudden or rash decision, but had sought guidance from the Lord, who curiously might lead men in different directions. Thus the parliamentarian John Hodgson recalled that he spent 'many an hour and night to seek God to know my way', while the royalist Sir William Campion sought guidance 'daily in my prayers for two or three months together to God to direct me in the right way'. The duty owed their divinely appointed monarch loomed large for some. Sir Edmund Verney stressed his loyalty to Charles, writing that 'my conscience is only concerned with honour and gratitude for to follow my master. I have eaten his bread and served

In some of his writings the puritan preacher Richard Baxter analysed the causes of the civil war and acknowledged that there could be differences between on the one hand the major issues at the centre, such as the dispute between king and parliament over control of the armed forces, which had led to the breakdown and the outbreak of war, and on the other hand those factors which motivated individuals to take up arms and to fight. Baxter claimed that for him and for many of his colleagues, the latter involved questions of religion, faith and liberty, brought into sharp focus by the consequences of the Irish rebellion. (Ann Ronan Picture Library)

him near thirty years, and will not do so base a thing as to forsake him, and choose rather to give my life – which I am sure I shall do.' His prediction came true, for he was cut down during the first major battle of the war. Sir Bevil Grenville explained that he joined Charles because 'I cannot contain myself indoors, when the king of England's standard waves in the field', Sir George Goring because 'I had it all from his Majesty, and he hath it all again'.

There survives a detailed letter from Sir Thomas Salusbury to his sister, written in late June on his way home after presenting his services to the king at York and being commissioned colonel of a yet-to-be-raised regiment. Salusbury explained that he had decided to serve Charles only after a period of soul-searching. He had studied the bible and biblical injunctions to 'fear God and honour the king' and to 'give unto Caesar the things that are Caesar's and unto God those things which belong to God', and had concluded that it was his Christian duty to serve his king. Conversely, he had been sickened by the stance of the king's opponents, 'the filthie dreamers of these times', men who 'defile the flesh, despise dominion and speake evill of Dignities'. They were already allowing the true religion to be corrupted by schism and heresy and if they were able to continue they would plunge the kingdom into the sort of religious turmoil, prolonged warfare, blood-letting and anarchy which had been seen on the continent over the previous decades and which inevitably resulted when a people withdrew obedience from their sovereign.

However, religious motivation could cut both ways, and historians have suggested that many of the parliamentarian enthusiasts who did not waiver, but who took up arms and were active from the outset, were driven forward by their faith. A radical Protestantism or puritanism, combined with a belief that their church was menaced by Catholic plots, marked out some of the parliamentary firebrands of the opening stages of the war, men like Oliver Cromwell and Sir William Brereton, who took up arms

at the outset, even though neither appears to have had any previous military experience. Writing a decade or so after the war had ended, the puritan divine Richard Baxter also claimed that he and many of his colleagues had been moved to fight by religious developments. In particular, Baxter had been sickened by the alleged collusion of the king and his ilk in the Irish rebellion, their friendship with the Irish Catholic party which 'barbarously murdered' and 'suddenly butchered' so many Protestants in Ireland and which was likely to overrun England. Charles was actively encouraging, or would soon have become a pawn in, this process, for 'his impious and popish armies would have ruled him'. On these grounds, Baxter said that he and many of his acquaintances had been impelled to support parliament.

It is clear that during the opening phase of the conflict there were some geographical patterns to allegiance and support. Some areas displayed marked enthusiasm for either king or parliament and provided large numbers of volunteers. These patterns of unforced, popular allegiance are often hard to reconstruct and interpret. In a few areas, community allegiance may have been determined by pre-war disputes and the pursuit of practical gain. For example, some of the miners in the Forest of Dean and parts of Derbyshire probably supported the king in the hope that he, in turn, would help them in their long-running disputes against local grandees. More broadly, in some regions, such as the western counties of Somerset, Wiltshire and Dorset, and the west Midlands in and around Warwickshire, a case has been made for communities splitting along pre-war lines of cleavage, rooted in a concoction of differing religious, economic, social and cultural outlooks. Within these areas, arable and mixed farming regions of downs and vales, of small parishes and nucleated settlements tightly controlled by church and resident squire, tended towards a traditional, conservative outlook and to royalist allegiance in the civil war, while wood-pasture and upland grazing regions, of large parishes, dispersed settlements and much weaker elite control, tended towards more open, fluid populations receptive to new ideas, who supported parliament when civil war broke out. However, these divisions are not so apparent in other parts of England and Wales and this interpretation does not explain emerging allegiances in many other regions. In some areas a case can be made for religion as a major element in determining allegiance. Those communities which favoured further reform of the state church, such as ports, many towns and cloth-working areas, were more likely to support parliament, while those which were ecclesiastically conservative and less reform-minded, including fairly isolated communities remote from transport highways, moorlands and large parts of the highland zone of England and Wales, the northern and western regions remote from the controversies in Whitehall and Westminster, were more likely to support the king. It has also been suggested that popular royalism in Wales and Cornwall in 1642 may have owed something to the historical, cultural and linguistic distinctiveness of those two non-English parts of the Celtic fringe. The royal principality of Wales came out for Charles in summer 1642, providing thousands of recruits who served as the backbone of the infantry in his first army, while in the royal duchy of Cornwall there was a popular royalist rising in October 1642, perhaps 10,000-strong, which secured that county for the king. It may be that the population in these areas felt that their distinctiveness would be threatened by an antagonistic parliament in London, where the press was increasingly condemning them as backward and suspiciously 'Popish' in outlook, and that their ways and rights, their distinctive Welsh and Cornish particularism, would be better protected by the king.

Several traits are apparent in the two armies which gathered in autumn 1642. Firstly, the senior ranks were dominated by men who had previous military experience. It has been estimated that, of those present at Edgehill, at least 60 parliamentarian and 30 royalist officers had fought on the Continent over the previous decades. Although the Stuart kingdoms had largely remained at peace during the opening decades of the 17th century, untold numbers of English and Welsh men, both elite and non-elite, as well as large numbers of Scots – one historian has put the figure at around 25,000 Scots in total, perhaps 10 per cent of that country's adult male population – had seen service abroad during the Thirty Years' War, fighting as volunteers or mercenaries. Secondly, there was a conspicuous number of Scottish officers, particularly on the parliamentary side. Thirdly, the two overall commanders, Charles I and the Earl of Essex, had far less experience than most of those directly under them; Charles I had none, for he had not led troops in person during the French or Spanish wars of the late 1620s or the Scots' Wars of 1639–40, while the parliamentary lord general had some experience as a colonel in the Dutch infantry during the 1620s as well as in the Scots' Wars. Fourthly, most senior commanders were men of fairly mature years, into middle age in a 17th- century context; indeed , several, particularly on the royalist side, were rather long in the tooth by 1642. Assessment of royalist and parliamentary armies later in war confirm this trend, showing that most officers ranked colonel and above were in their 30s or 40s.

The English civil war, 1642–46

The armies

The infantry formed the core of the civil war army and was generally the largest of its three main elements. Foot soldiers were either musketeers or pikemen. Musketeers, who usually wore no body armour, had swords and could use their muskets as clubs in close-quarter combat or when they ran out of ammunition. Thus at Naseby, Fairfax's musketeers attacked an obstinate unit of royalist foot 'with Butt-end of Muskets and so broke them'. However, the musketeer's principal role was to fire on the enemy using his musket. This had a long barrel, probably around four feet or so at the start of the war (though rather shorter, lighter muskets were soon introduced) and fired a spherical lead bullet. In flintlock or 'firelock' muskets, the charge was ignited by a mechanism that brought a flint down against a piece of steel, producing a spark. In matchlock muskets, a slow-burning length of cord ignited the powder. There were obvious dangers in the musketeer carrying a burning match when he was also handling gunpowder, the match needed attention to ensure that it was burning evenly, it was hard to keep alight in rain and its glow might give away troop positions at night. However, matchlock muskets were cheaper to produce than flintlocks, their firing mechanism was simpler and they could often still be fired even if that mechanism broke. Accordingly, the matchlock was the standard-issue weapon through the English civil wars. Musketeers carried their ammunition on a bandolier, a leather belt worn across the shoulder, from which hung both a number

The mechanism of a flintlock or 'firelock' musket of the civil wars, in which a flint was brought down against a steel arm when the trigger was pulled, producing sparks. This type of musket did not require a burning match, and so was often used by troops protecting supplies of gunpowder or by those undertaking surprise night-time raids. (Royal Armouries)

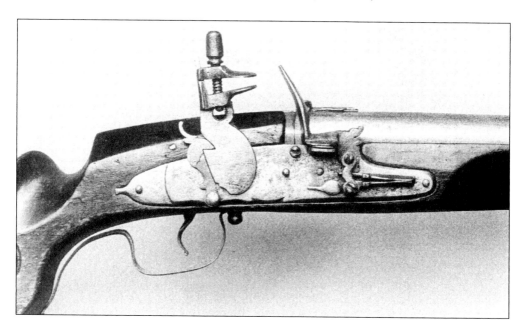

The mechanism of a matchlock musket of the civil wars. The smouldering match would be held in the rather ornate 'serpent' which, when the trigger was pulled, would lower the match into the priming pan. Just before firing the musketeer would swivel open the pan cover, thus exposing the charge of powder in the pan. (Royal Armouries)

of powder containers holding the main charges and a separate bag of musket balls. Later in the war, some troops began using cartridges, rolls of paper each containing a measure of gunpowder and a ball, which could be rammed up the barrel in one go, instead of loading powder and ball separately. The musketeer also carried a priming flask containing gunpowder, a small amount of which was tipped into an externally-opening firing pan; when ignited, this served to light the main charge. Muskets were not particularly accurate – they had a theoretical range of up to 400 yards but an effective range well below that – and could only fire one shot at a time before needing to be reloaded. Accordingly musketeers worked together, firing roughly aimed volleys by rank into blocks of enemy troops. They often operated in revolving ranks, with the front rank firing their volley and then retiring to the rear to begin the process of reloading. By the time they had completed this the rank in front of them had reloaded, presented, fired and retired, and so on. The number of ranks employed varied, depending on the numbers of men available and the length of time they were taking to reload, but was generally between three and six, arranged so that between them they could maintain an almost constant hail of

shot. An experienced musketeer could reload and fire in well under a minute.

The pikemen also fought together in distinct blocks. Although their use of body armour was declining, at the time of the English civil wars most pikemen probably wore armour to protect the torso and thighs, and a simple pot-style, rounded helmet. Some also had a gorget to protect the neck and back of the head. Many carried a sword slung from the waist, but their principal weapon was their pike, a long wooden stave about 16 feet in length and tipped with a steel point. Sometimes the fighting end had long, thin steel plates attached to it to give it extra strength. A block of pikemen, their pikes pointing outwards like a giant hedgehog, could advance at a steady pace and engage the enemy directly, hoping either to break them outright or to fight opposing pikemen at close quarters in a form of stabbing, prodding melee that was generally referred to as 'push of pike'. Their main role, however, was to resist and break up cavalry attacks and to protect their own musketeers from enemy horse. Thus in battle, in which the infantry as a whole normally occupied the centre of the deployed army, blocks of musketeers and pikemen would be interspersed, with units of pikemen flanking and protecting adjoining units of musketeers. During the opening phase of the war, many armies contained roughly equal numbers of musketeers and pikemen, but it was generally thought that the ideal arrangement was to have a preponderance of musketeers over pikemen, in a ratio of three to two or two to one. Later

The equipment of a mounted harquebusier, including a leather buff coat, armour protecting the chest and the bridle arm, an open-fronted helmet and, carried at his side and attached to belts across both shoulders, a broadsword and a carbine. (Royal Armouries)

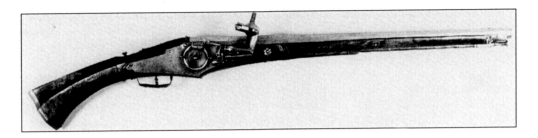

in the war musketeers did significantly outnumber pikemen in most of the principal field armies.

While infantry occupied a central position on the battlefield, cavalry took up position either side of it, holding the wings. Some cavalry wore full, three-quarter-length body armour, from an enclosed helmet down to just below the knees. A few units of this sort, known as cuirassiers, fought in the civil wars, notably a parliamentary unit under Sir Arthur Heselrige, famously described by Clarendon as 'so prodigiously armed that they were called by the other side the regiment of lobsters because of the bright iron shells with which they were covered'. This style of cavalry was rapidly going out of fashion, as the armour was expensive and heavy, making it very difficult for a cuirassier to manoeuvre or to remount in battle, and by the mid-17th century it was not entirely musket-proof.

A pair of flintlock pistols of the civil wars. These were the type of pistol used by most civil war cavalrymen, typically carried in holsters on either side of the horse, immediately in front of the saddle. (National Army Museum)

A wheellock pistol of the civil wars. The spark was produced when a piece of pyrites was held against the revolving serrated wheel. The wheel was first wound back against a spring, using a spanner or key which fitted onto the nut in the centre of the wheel. (National Army Museum)

Thus the great majority of civil war cavalry were the faster, lighter, more manoeuvrable harquebusiers, who wore far less body armour. This might comprise a three-quarter-length buff coat of thick leather, which offered some protection from sword blows, or metal back and breast plates to protect the upper torso, and perhaps a metal gauntlet protecting the bridle arm from elbow to knuckle. They generally wore an open-style metal helmet, with one or more bars protecting the face. It was impractical for cavalry to use full muskets on horseback, but they were sometimes armed with a shorter version called a carbine, which typically had a barrel between 2 and $2^{1}/_{2}$ feet long and which hung by the cavalryman's side, attached by a clip to a bandolier passing over his shoulder. A carbine was fired either by a flintlock

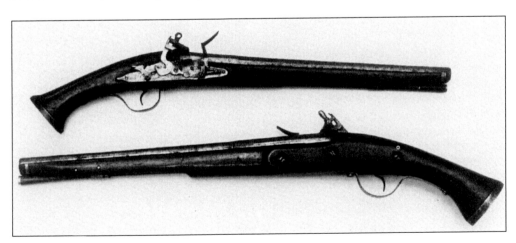

mechanism or by a wheellock, in which a serrated wheel was wound back against a spring using a spanner and, when released, revolved against a piece of pyrites fixed over the firing pan, producing a shower of sparks. The flintlock mechanism was generally cheaper and more reliable.

The cavalryman normally had a brace of pistols, carried in holsters on either side in front of the saddle, typically with a barrel length of 14–15 inches and again fired by either the flintlock or wheellock mechanism. In the heat of battle, a carbine or pistol might be fired just once, as there was limited opportunity to reload, and officers tried to ensure that their men were as close as possible to the enemy before firing. However, the principal cavalryman's weapon was his sword, with a steel blade and iron hilt, carried in a scabbard and worn from a belt which went either round the waist or across the shoulder. Various types of sword were used, including narrow, probing rapiers, but typically cavalry used a wide-bladed, slashing broadsword. Thus armed, cavalry served as the shock troops of a civil war army, able to move forward at speed in units often three ranks deep, sometimes slowing to fire as they approached the enemy, sometimes just charging on in the hope of smashing, breaking open or carrying away the enemy lines, reserving their fire until after the initial impact.

The third element of an army, the dragoons, were essentially foot soldiers, but they had horses, often poor-quality mounts, which enabled them to ride forward and take up advanced positions. Typically they would be employed to secure, occupy or clear particular strong points between the two main armies, such as hedges and ditches, walls, gates and bridges. They would then dismount and fight on foot from these forward positions, firing on and disrupting advancing enemy forces. They generally wore little body armour and were equipped with swords and either muskets or carbines with flintlock or wheellock mechanisms so that they did not have to use matches and would be able to fire from horseback if necessary.

A number of other symbolic or functional weapons saw very limited use in the armies of the English civil wars, including poleaxes, halberds, bills and blunderbusses. Standard muskets and carbines were not very accurate, but more expensive and accurate birding or fowling pieces were available and would be given to snipers to pick off specific targets, though this was more common in sieges than field engagements. Most of the bigger armies took with them a train of artillery, including very large, heavy and slow-moving cannon, though again these were more suited to sieges than battles. But other pieces were shorter, lighter and more mobile and these, typically firing iron balls weighing less than 10 pounds, might play a more substantial role in battle. Many of the major engagements opened with an artillery exchange, firing at a fairly sedate rate, as reloading was slow and complex. They made a great deal of noise and smoke and could inflict terrible injuries. There are plenty of gory contemporary accounts of the damage done to the human body, of 'legs and arms flying apace', of 'a whole file of men, six deep, with their heads struck off with one cannon shot', of 'guts lying on the ground'. On the other hand, many contemporaries also noted that the cannons generally 'caused more terror than execution', that 'their cannon did very small execution amongst us' and that 'great artillery seldom or never hurts'. Civil war battles were decided by the clash of horse and foot, not by an exchange of artillery.

Infantry and cavalry were organised into, and fought as, larger units of men. A foot soldier was a member of a company, generally commanded by a captain, which at this time should have numbered around or a little over 100–120 men. Infantry companies were gathered together into a regiment under the overall command of a colonel, who had his own regimental officers. Ideally an infantry regiment would be made up of 10 companies and so would number somewhere over 1,000 men. In practice, the strength of individual companies varied widely during the course of the war and often fell way short of 100. Similarly the number of companies that made up an infantry regiment also varied, from just a handful up to the mid or high teens.

A cavalryman was a member of a troop of horse. In the early phase of the war, a troop often numbered around 60 ordinary troopers and about 10 officers and staff, including the commanding officer, generally a captain. As the war progressed, troop size often increased, and troops of 80–90 or more became fairly common on parliament's side, less so on the king's, though again numbers could fluctuate wildly between good times and bad. Although the organisation was incomplete when the two armies met at Edgehill, both sides soon grouped their troops of horse into cavalry regiments, generally commanded by a colonel. The number of troops to a regiment was never completely standardised and although six or seven became something like the norm, there were exceptions. In 1643 Oliver Cromwell commanded a double horse regiment of 14 troops, and at one point Prince Rupert's regiment had 10 troops. Thus although a horse regiment of six or seven troops might number somewhere between 400 and 500 men, it could be very much larger or smaller.

Raw recruits needed basic training before they could safely join a field army and take part in battle. Drawing upon their own experience of fighting and a variety of military and drill manuals, the officers (often corporals) in charge of new recruits would train the men to respond individually and together to a range of standard commands. These would entail not only personal movements, such as marching, turning, wheeling and so forth, but also the handling of their weapons. If mishandled, the sharp and butt ends of a pike could do considerable damage to colleagues in their own company. The musket was potentially even more lethal, to its owner as much as to his colleagues around him, and the complex procedure for loading, firing and reloading, involving the handling of gunpowder and a burning match, as well as the cleaning of the weapons, called for careful training. If that training proved inadequate, the results could be devastating. In autumn

A bust of Charles I's nephew, Prince Rupert, portraying him in the late 1670s, towards the end of his life. In 1642, Rupert, then a dashing 23-year-old, but already with military experience and a reputation for courage and boldness gained while serving on the Continent in the later 1630s, was appointed general of the horse in his uncle's army. (Topham Picturepoint)

1642 at the battle of Edgehill 'a careless soldier in fetching powder where a magazine was, clapped his hand carelessly into a barrel of powder with his match between his fingers, whereby much powder was blown up and many killed'. In November 1643 a unit of parliamentary musketeers attacking Basing House were woefully inexperienced, and instead of firing by rank, they all fired together, so that some in the front were shot by their colleagues behind them.

Intense basic training for infantry recruits could be completed in a week. Once they were proficient in handling their weapons and had been taken through their 'postures' in companies, they would be brought together as a new regiment or join and reinforce an existing regiment, whereupon they would receive instruction from more senior officers in battlefield formations and tactics. The training of cavalry was broadly similar, entailing the handling of weapons, individual manoeuvres on horseback and then working together as a troop on its own and within a regiment, practising different movements. In addition, the horses needed their own training so that they became accustomed to the sight and sounds of gunfire and would not panic and run out of control on the battlefield. But however thorough the drill and training on the parade ground, most veterans felt that nothing could beat the experience of real action and that, until they had been blooded in their first battle, new recruits were always something of a liability.

The principal campaigns

When the English civil wars began in August 1642 many people expected the conflict to

be brief, with each side raising a single army which would then crash into each other with everything resolved in one dreadful but decisive battle. Looking back, Richard Baxter ruefully recalled 'that we commonly supposed that in a very few days or weeks one Battle would end the war'. It would all be over by Christmas. Indeed, events initially followed that course, for king and parliament did focus much of their efforts on raising two large field armies, which, after a period of manoeuvring in the West Midlands, crashed into each other in

The movements of the main royalist and parliamentary armies during the opening weeks of the war, culminating in the battle of Edgehill of 23 October 1642.

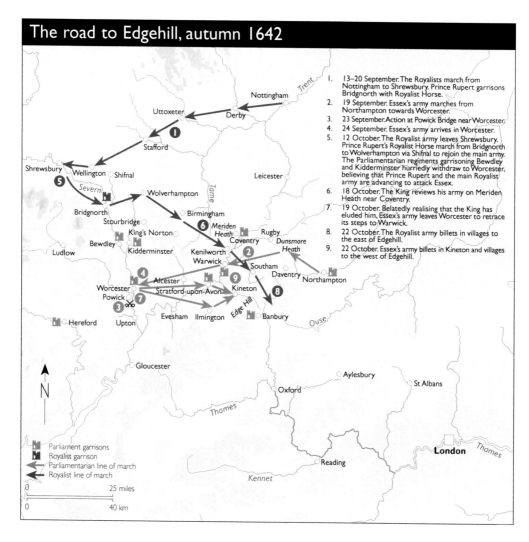

The road to Edgehill, autumn 1642

1. 13–20 September. The Royalists march from Nottingham to Shrewsbury. Prince Rupert garrisons Bridgnorth with Royalist Horse.
2. 19 September. Essex's army marches from Northampton towards Worcester.
3. 23 September. Action at Powick Bridge near Worcester.
4. 24 September. Essex's army arrives in Worcester.
5. 12 October. The Royalist army leaves Shrewsbury. Prince Rupert's Royalist Horse march from Bridgnorth to Wolverhampton via Shifnal to rejoin the main army. The Parliamentarian regiments garrisoning Bewdley and Kidderminster hurriedly withdraw to Worcester, believing that Prince Rupert and the main Royalist army are advancing to attack Essex.
6. 18 October. The King reviews his army on Meriden Heath near Coventry.
7. 19 October. Belatedly realising that the King has eluded him, Essex's army leaves Worcester to retrace its steps to Warwick.
8. 22 October. The Royalist army billets in villages to the east of Edgehill.
9. 22 October. Essex's army billets in Kineton and villages to the west of Edgehill.

Parliament garrisons
Royalist garrison
Parliamentarian line of march
Royalist line of march

0   25 miles

0   40 km

Warwickshire. During September the king moved from Nottingham to Shrewsbury, to rendezvous with recruits from Wales and parts of the Welsh Marches as well as those marching south from Lancashire. The Earl of Essex meanwhile led his growing army first to Northampton and then west to Worcester, to block Charles should he move down the Severn valley. There were skirmishes between detached units, the largest of which occurred on 23 September 1642 when parliamentary and royalist horse clashed around Powick Bridge, south of Worcester, ahead of the arrival of Essex's main army, with the king's men gaining a clear victory.

With a now much stronger army, the king left Shrewsbury on 12 October, but he swung south-east, as if to take a Midlands route towards London. Somewhat tardily, Essex realised what was afoot and moved his army east out of Worcester on 19 October to intercept the king. By the evening of the 22nd they were on Charles' heels on the Warwickshire plain and the king decided to turn and give battle. During Sunday 23 October the two armies drew up opposite each other, with infantry in the centre, horse on both wings, and dragoons on the two flanks. The king's army initially gathered on top of Edgehill, but when it became clear that Essex would not attack uphill, he brought his army down to deploy along the base of the hill, while Essex deployed on a slight ridge in the plain below. Like many major civil war engagements, battle took place by mutual consent.

The two armies, around 13–14,000 men apiece, faced each other in matching, parallel lines, under a mile apart. Battle began in the afternoon with an inconclusive artillery exchange and skirmishes between dragoons. Then the royalist cavalry on both wings charged forward and engaged the parliamentary horse, who, receiving them stationary and firing a not very effective volley, quickly buckled, broke, fell back and turned away in full flight. But instead of halting, rallying and turning to attack the parliamentary infantry, most of the victorious royalist horse – both the main line and a second line intended as the reserve – swept on in pursuit of the fleeing parliamentary cavalry and Essex's baggage train. The royalist infantry was thus left with little cavalry support as it moved forward to engage the parliamentary foot, which was bolstered by a couple of cavalry units that had been kept in reserve and had not been swept away. The parliamentary horse overran and put out of action much of the royalist artillery. Aided by cavalry support and probably with superior firepower, the parliamentary infantry had the better of a dour, often close-quarter fight with the royalist foot, pushing the king's men back and for a time capturing the royal standard, though it was later recovered. A mixture of exhaustion, dwindling powder supplies and nightfall brought proceedings to an inconclusive close, with neither side securing a clear victory. Had Rupert and the victorious front line of royalist horse not careered off the battlefield, and had the second line not joined them but remained on the battlefield as a reserve, the outcome might have been very different.

There followed an unseasonably cold night, which may have saved some of the wounded by helping to stem their loss of blood, but probably finished others off through exposure. Denzil Holles recalled that 'We almost starved with cold that bitter night', while Edmund Ludlow wrote that, having found some bread, 'I could scarce eat it, my jaws for want of use having almost lost their natural faculty', a symptom which one historian has ascribed to the intense clenching of teeth of post-combat trauma. The two sides eyed each other suspiciously on the following day, but were too drained to resume battle and eventually both pulled back. Essex went northwards to Warwick, Charles south-eastwards, resuming his march towards Banbury and in the general direction of London. They left a total of over 1,000 dead on and around the battlefield, some quickly buried in situ by their colleagues, others buried there or in nearby churchyards by the local population.

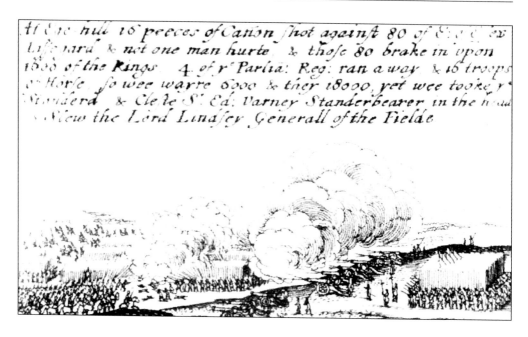

ff the hull 16 peeces of Canon shot against 80 of ... Life ...ard & not one man hurte & those 80 brake in upon 1600 of the kings. 4 of y Parlia: Reg: ran away & 16 troops ... Horse so wee warre 6000 & ther 18000, yet wee tooke y Standerd & Clete S Ed: Varney Standerbearer in the h... Slew the Lord Linasey Generall of the Fielde

A contemporary image of fighting at Edgehill, showing artillery fire, blocks of pikemen and cavalry in action. The inscription reveals the parliamentary origins and bias of the engraving, stressing the ineffectiveness of the royalist attack and the deaths of two prominent royalist officers. (Public domain)

Over the following fortnight the king moved slowly, capturing Banbury, spending a pleasant time in Oxford and marching via Reading before finally approaching London from the west around 9 November. By then, Essex had brought his army back to London, where it was bolstered by the London trained bands, rapidly growing as Londoners flocked to defend the capital, and by up to seven newly raised regiments. On 12 November the royalists launched a fierce attack on Brentford, smashing two parliamentary infantry regiments and causing much death and destruction. This brutality strengthened the resolve of the parliamentary soldiers and civilians to defend the capital, and it may also have left Charles uneasy and disinclined to unleash further bloodshed. On the following day, 13 November, he found his route to London blocked at Turnham Green by a huge force of over 24,000 parliamentarians and, having glared at his enemies all day, he decided not to give battle but pull away under cover of darkness. Even though he

significantly outnumbered the royalists, Essex chose not to pursue the king or try to force battle. Many historians suggest that had the king quickly marched on London after Edgehill and attacked it before the main parliamentary army had returned there, Charles might have captured the capital and perhaps thereby won the war in autumn 1642.

Thus the civil war did not end quickly for the campaign of autumn 1642 had proved indecisive, and it became clear that war would stretch into and through 1643 and perhaps beyond. During the depth of winter 1642–43, as during most winters of the war, military action dwindled but did not entirely cease. But because of the weather and the state of the roads, it was generally impossible to mount major campaigns, fighting slackened off and the main armies went into winter quarters. In December 1642 the king fell back to Oxford, which became his headquarters for the remainder of the war, and his army quartered in and around the town, protected by a circuit of outlying bases. Essex quartered his army in an arc west of London. Winter was the season of preparation for the looming campaign, for building up resources, and often for abortive peace talks, such as the rather desultory ones between king and parliament in Oxford early in 1643 focused upon a set of terms called the Oxford Propositions.

The winter of 1642–43 also saw a change in the nature of the war, from building up and resourcing two principal field armies to securing the towns and countryside of England and Wales, gaining territory and the demographic, financial and material resources that could be taken from it. On both sides, determined military leaders backed by troops and civilian commissioners moved to quell or cut through the uncertainty and apathy of the opening months of the war, to override the various neutrality pacts that had been concluded between parliamentary and royalist activists in many areas and to force the whole country to swing behind king or parliament and begin supplying the manpower for a potentially lengthy civil war. Territory was tied down and its resources secured by establishing garrisons – bodies of troops stationed to control an area. By spring 1643 it was possible to draw a map of England and Wales showing how the two sides had secured and carved up territory in this way. Although the allegiance of some areas was unclear and disputed, the overall pattern was apparent by May 1643. In terms of area, the two sides held roughly equal territories at this stage, but parliament held the richer and more populous parts of the country, most of the major ports (Plymouth, Exeter, Bristol, Portsmouth, London, Boston, Hull and Milford Haven, though not Newcastle) and all three of the biggest pre-war arsenals (Portsmouth, London and Hull).

During 1643 the war became a far more intense and inevitably long-drawn-out territorial conflict, fought by a diversity of principal, provincial and local armies and by large numbers of soldiers in hundreds of garrisons. Both sides intensified their war efforts, raising large numbers of voluntary or conscripted recruits, probably a total of something approaching 150,000 men at the height of the 1643 campaigning season. In many ways 1643 was also the most complex year of the war, with fighting in many parts of England and Wales. However, an overall pattern slowly emerged. 1643 was a year of repeated royalist successes and substantial territorial gains, which pushed the parliamentarians back to their heartlands in the south-eastern quarter of England. It is not clear whether Charles had consciously conceived a plan at the beginning of 1643 for a three-pronged attack on London. Nevertheless, the royalists undoubtedly expanded and advanced in the south, the north and the Midlands during the year, and London became far more vulnerable.

The most dramatic royalist progress was made in the south and south-west, though from a slow and frustrating start. At the beginning of 1643 the king alone held Cornwall and the royalists found it hard to break out. On 19 January parliamentary forces were badly mauled on Boconnoc or Braddock Down, but a royalist attempt to push into Devon fizzled out. Again in late April, after repulsing a parliamentary attack on Launceston, the Cornish royalists tried but failed to push east and were thrown back to Sourton Down on the night of 25–26 April. But on 16 May Sir Ralph Hopton crushed parliament's south-western army in battle outside Stratton, scoring a decisive victory against the Earl of Stamford's parliamentarians who were both numerically stronger and held a hill-top position. The king began pouring reinforcements into the area and gained significant territory. Advancing eastwards, the royalists encountered parliament's main southern army under Sir William Waller in early July. Although the first clash, on Lansdown Hill outside Bath on 5 July, was indecisive, at Roundway Down on 13 July a reinforced royalist army destroyed Waller's army and the region opened up for the king. During the summer, royalists secured a huge swathe of territory across the west country and southern England, including Devon, Dorset, Somerset, most of Gloucestershire, Wiltshire and the western half of Hampshire, capturing the great town and port of

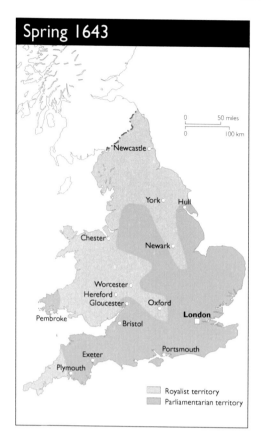

Spring 1643

Newcastle

0   50 miles

0   100 km

York   Hull

Chester

Newark

Worcester
Hereford
Gloucester   Oxford

Pembroke   **London**

Bristol

Portsmouth

Exeter

Plymouth

Royalist territory
Parliamentarian territory

England and Wales divided, spring 1643. The king held the north of England, parts of the north west (most of Lancashire and part of western Cheshire), almost the whole of Wales (but not Pembrokeshire), the far south-west (Cornwall) and a tongue of territory extending from the central Marches, across much of the West Midlands, to Oxfordshire. Parliament had secured the rest.

Bristol on 26 July. There were some disappointments. A few towns, such as Plymouth and Lyme Regis, held out for parliament and a prolonged royalist siege of Gloucester failed, thwarted by determined resistance and bad weather. The king abandoned the operation on 5 September at the approach of a relieving army of 15,000 raised around London and led by Essex. At Newbury on 20 September the king tried but failed to block this army's return to London. The first battle of Newbury, the biggest engagement of 1643 with around 13–15,000 men on each side, was confused and indecisive, ending at nightfall with the king pulling back to Oxford and Essex able to continue his march.

In northern England royalist forces also gained ground under William Cavendish,

Contemporary portraits of the parliamentarian Sir William Waller by Cornelius Johnson (left) and the royalist Sir Ralph Hopton, later Baron Hopton of Stratton (right), by an unknown artist. The two men clashed several times in southern England during the opening year or so of the war, most notably at the battle of Lansdown in July 1643 and again at Cheriton in March 1644. They were old friends and sought to preserve that friendship, maintaining a warm correspondence throughout the war. Waller's letter to Hopton is an eloquent and oft-quoted expression of the disdain with which a few went to war. Waller regretted 'this present distance between us', stressed that 'my affections to you are so unchangeable, that hostility itself cannot violate my friendship to your person' and reflected upon 'what a sad sense I go upon this service, and with what a perfect hatred I detest this war without an enemy... We are both upon the stage and must act those parts assigned us in this tragedy. Let us do it in a way of honour, and without personal animosities, whatever the issue be'. (National Portrait Gallery)

Earl of Newcastle. He entered York in December 1642 with an army of over 8,000 men and sought to secure the whole county. During early 1643 royalist control of southern and western Yorkshire was disputed by parliamentary forces under Ferdinando, Baron Fairfax, and his son, Sir Thomas Fairfax. They harried the king's forces and

Sir Thomas Fairfax, one of the most successful parliamentary officers of the opening years of the civil war, became lord general and commander-in-chief of the parliamentary armies in spring 1645, a position he retained until he resigned his command in summer 1650. This contemporary engraving, which appeared in Joshua Sprigge's *Anglia Rediviva* (published in 1647), also depicts in the background, below Fairfax's horse, blocks of pikemen and units of horse marching or deploying. (Bridgeman Art Library) scored some notable triumphs, storming Leeds on 23 January and raiding Wakefield on 21 May. But the royalists' numerical and material advantages slowly told. On 30 March, Sir Thomas Fairfax lost many men in a running fight with George Goring's royalists when he tried to make a stand on Seacroft Moor, and on 30 June 1643 Newcastle's main army, around 10,000 strong, crushed the Fairfaxes and their army of 4,000 men on Adwalton Moor outside Bradford.

By then, some northern royalist forces were pushing into Lincolnshire. Newark had been secured for the king at the end of 1642 and was being developed into a huge base. The Lincolnshire parliamentarians came under increasing pressure during 1643 and were forced back, though they mounted strong resistance and for a time fortunes ebbed and flowed. Thus on 23 March royalists stormed and captured Grantham and on 11 April they brushed aside a small parliamentary army on Ancaster Heath. However, parliamentary forces retook Grantham in early May and on 13 May they mauled royalists around Belton. In mid-July the parliamentarians captured Gainsborough and on 28 July they attacked and repulsed an army sent to retake the town. But the arrival of royalist reinforcements tipped the balance decisively and by the end of the summer the king controlled most of Lincolnshire, the parliamentarians being forced back into the south. That they had held out for so long was due to their own determination and to Newcastle's division of his forces, for he did not commit much of his army to Lincolnshire. Instead, during the late summer and early autumn he undertook a long and fruitless siege of Hull. Abandoned in mid-October, this operation divided royalist resources and weakened the drive south. Many historians compare Newcastle's failed operation against Hull to Charles's equally abortive siege of Gloucester and condemn both as grave mistakes, wasting time and dividing resources which should have been focused on a royalist push towards London.

The war in the Midlands during 1643 was also confused, and although the king's men again won the upper hand, royalist territorial advances were not as dramatic. Indeed, around the fringes parliamentary forces gained some notable successes early in the campaigning season. Thus Sir John Gell captured Lichfield for parliament in March, and the Earl of Essex Reading on 27 April. During the spring Sir William Waller led a short but successful campaign in the southern Marches, routing an inexperienced Welsh army at Highnam on 24 March and seizing Hereford on 25 April. But the tide turned. Parliamentary forces in Staffordshire were heavily defeated in battle on Hopton Heath, outside Stafford, on 19 March, and Prince Rupert recovered Lichfield on 20 April. Waller's forces had been badly shaken by Prince Maurice's royalists at Ripple, north of Tewkesbury, on 13 April, even before they captured Hereford, and royalist pressure there and elsewhere caused Waller to abandon Hereford itself and fall back in late May; he and his men were needed to try to hold Somerset and Wiltshire. Sparring between the two sides in the Home Counties and fringing royalist Oxfordshire was less decisive but generally turned in the royalists' favour, including an otherwise minor encounter at Chalgrove on 18 June in which the widely respected parliamentarian, John Hampden, perished. After the first battle of Newbury, Essex abandoned Reading and pulled back to protect the increasingly vulnerable capital.

By the end of the 1643 campaign the royalists were in the ascendant. Parliament had been forced back into its heartlands of London, the south-east, East Anglia and parts of the East Midlands, with a now insecure salient running across the North Midlands to the north west. Even that core territory appeared threatened. By winter 1643–44 the king held over two-thirds of England and Wales and appeared to be winning the war. However, by spring 1644 the tide was turning. Forced back into defending their heartlands, the parliamentarians focused their resources and started winning important engagements. On 11 October they defeated a larger royalist force at Winceby in southern Lincolnshire, thus halting the advance southwards of the northern royalists. In mid-September an attempt to take and hold King's Lynn for the king was crushed. In December Sir Ralph Hopton tried to move eastwards into Sussex, but he was rebuffed by Waller, who quickly recovered Chichester and the town and castle of Arundel, and the royalist invasion fizzled out. On 13 December Waller had also retaken Alton in north-east Hampshire, closing another possible line of royalist advance. On 29 March Waller and Hopton clashed again at Cheriton, in south-east Hampshire. The royalists were badly mauled and forced back with heavy losses. The advance of the royalists eastwards through southern England had been turned back.

The changing fortunes of king and parliament also owed much to the involvement of allies. During 1643 the king concluded a truce or cessation with the Irish Catholic rebels, allowing him to ship men over to fight for him in England and Wales. The first batch of troops began landing on the Welsh side of the Dee estuary during the closing weeks of 1643, in the process ending a brief campaign by Sir William Brereton's forces to push around the western side of royalist Chester. These newly landed forces launched a short but brutal mid-winter campaign to clear Cheshire of parliamentarians, but on 25 January, as they were besieging Nantwich, they were attacked and destroyed by a relieving force led across the Pennines by Fairfax. Thereafter, few further troops were brought across from Ireland, in part because the king wished to retain troops in Ireland, in part because parliament's naval supremacy blocked the Irish Sea crossing. The king's deal with the Irish Catholics brought him little military

A parliamentary propaganda image of the immediate aftermath of the battle of Marston Moor. Prince Rupert is shown hiding in a bean field near York. To the right, his dog 'Boye', a large hunting poodle, lies dead, and Rupert's baggage has been opened, revealing crucifixes and other Roman Catholic items. (Topham Picturepoint)

Autumn 1643

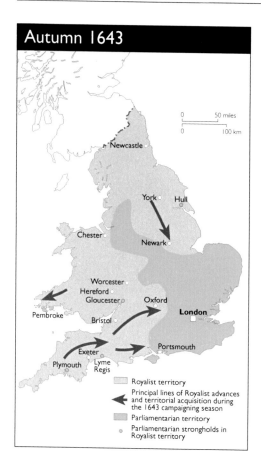

England and Wales divided, autumn 1643. By the end of the 1643 campaigning season parliament had been forced back into its heartlands of London, the south-east, East Anglia and parts of the East Midlands, with a now insecure salient running across the North Midlands to the north west.

gain and was a propaganda coup for parliament, which roundly condemned him for dealing with Catholic rebels who had so recently murdered Protestants. The limited number of troops that were brought across to the mainland were smeared as Irish Catholic murderers, even though in reality they were overwhelmingly English and Welsh Protestants who had gone over to Ireland in 1641–42 or were Irish Protestants who had taken up arms in self-protection. Charles struggled to get his message across but even many loyal supporters were deeply dismayed by his deal with the Irish Catholics.

Far more effective in every way was parliament's alliance with the Scottish

Covenanters, the Solemn League and Covenant of September 1643. In consequence, a Scottish army of over 22,000 men crossed the Tweed on 19 January 1644 and began rolling south, swatting away royalist forces and heading for York. The northern royalists, especially those in the king's northern capital, were squeezed between a large Scottish army and resurgent English parliamentary forces which joined together in a huge Anglo-Scottish siege operation. Dispatched north to relieve the city, Rupert swung through the north-west, smashing his way into Stockport and Bolton, securing Liverpool and picking up reinforcements, before swinging east to aid York. He eluded the main parliamentary army and successfully entered the city on 1 July, but he felt that his ambiguous instructions from the king and the military circumstances meant that he should give battle immediately. The ensuing engagement, fought on 2 July on the moorland of Marston Moor, was the largest battle of the first civil war of 1642–46, involving up to 28,000 English and Scottish parliamentarians and perhaps 18,000 royalists. During the day the two armies drew up in matching parallel lines, less than half a mile apart. At around 7 pm, during a rainstorm, the whole parliamentary line moved forward at speed. The infantry in the centre clashed indecisively, while the parliamentary cavalry on the right wing under Sir Thomas Fairfax found their advance hampered by the ground and were mauled. However, the parliamentary cavalry on the left under Oliver Cromwell broke the opposing royalist horse after a fierce fight and then, rather than careering off the battlefield, halted, turned and began tearing into the now exposed royalist foot. Repeated parliamentary attacks broke the remaining units of the royalist army and by 9 pm battle ended in a decisive victory for parliament and a disastrous defeat for the king. Rupert returned south soon after with the remnants of his army, Newcastle decided that his war was over and left the country, and the royalist position in northern England

Autumn 1644

Royalist territory

Royalist strongholds in Parliamentarian territory

Principal lines of Parliamentarian advances and territorial acquisition during the 1644 campaigning season

Parliamentarian territory

Parliamentarian strongholds in Royalist territory

England and Wales divided, autumn 1644. By the end of the 1644 campaigning season parliament had conquered almost the whole of northern England, with the royalists holding just a handful of isolated and doomed strongholds in that region. But in Wales, the Midlands and southern England, parliament had made little headway during 1644.

surrounded and forced to surrender en masse. When parliament's two principal southern commanders, Essex and Waller, failed to co-operate, the king seized the opportunity to outrun, outmanoeuvre and humiliate them separately. Waller pursued the king during June as he crossed and recrossed the southern Midlands, eventually closing in on him on 29 June in the Cherwell valley. Waller launched a two-pronged attack on the royalists around Cropredy Bridge but was savagely repulsed with heavy losses. Leaving Waller to struggle to hold together his shaken, depleted and mutinous army, the king turned west to deal

disintegrated. York surrendered later in July, the town of Newcastle in the autumn, and by the end of the year the royalists retained no more than a handful of isolated and doomed outposts in northern England.

Parliament had some successes in the Midlands and the south during 1644, including the capture of Montgomery in early September and on 18 September victory over a royalist army sent to recapture the town and castle. But these victories were more than offset by defeats. In March a parliamentary attack on the royalist base of Newark went disastrously wrong and the parliamentary army of 7,000 were repulsed,

England and Wales divided, autumn 1645. By the end of the 1645 campaigning season parliament was clearly winning the war and had captured extensive territory in southern England and south Wales. The king retained a scattering of isolated strongholds, islands of territory around Oxford and Newark, the far south-west and much of mid and north Wales.

Autumn 1645

Royalist territory

Royalist strongholds in Parliamentarian territory

Principal lines of Parliamentarian advances and territorial acquisition during the 1645 campaigning season

Parliamentarian territory

Parliamentarian strongholds in Royalist territory

with Essex, who was marching into the west country to relieve pressure on the besieged town and port of Lyme Regis. Having achieved this, he then marched his army further westwards during July and August, deeper into royalist territory and an ever-narrowing peninsula. Increasingly isolated and marooned and with the king in pursuit and running an effective campaign to dislodge him from possible strongholds, Essex ran out of territory. Well co-ordinated royalist action on 21 August forced Essex south out of Lostwithiel. On 31 August much of his cavalry managed to get away under cover of darkness to the relative safety of Plymouth, but there was no escape for the infantry

Robert Streeter's engraving of the battle of Naseby, from Sprigge's *Anglia Rediviva*, is one of very few surviving contemporary or near-contemporary depictions of a civil war engagement. More likely drawn on a visit to the battlefield sometime later rather than during the engagement itself, and so probably resting upon the memories of participants and witnesses and a degree of artistic licence, this is nonetheless a rare and very valuable representation of a major civil war engagement. (Heritage Images Partnership))

which surrendered en masse on 2 September. Essex's 'invasion' had turned into a fiasco and a disaster. The year ended no better; for by pressurising a string of royalist bases, such as Basing House and Donnington and Banbury Castles, the parliamentarians induced Charles to gather his southern forces around Newbury in October. By 26 October parliament had an army of over 16,000 men ready to pounce on the king's 9,500 men. But the parliamentarians were over-ambitious and divided their forces, sending part of their army on an overnight march to attack the far end of the king's line, and at the second battle of Newbury on 27 October the two parliamentary armies, now a couple of miles apart, failed to co-ordinate their attacks. Some parliamentary commanders appeared lethargic and the king was able to hold off his enemies and slip away almost unscathed at nightfall.

Unsuccessful peace negotiations resumed at Uxbridge early in 1645, focusing on a harsh and unrealistic set of Uxbridge Propositions. More importantly, in the wake of the military failures and disasters of 1644,

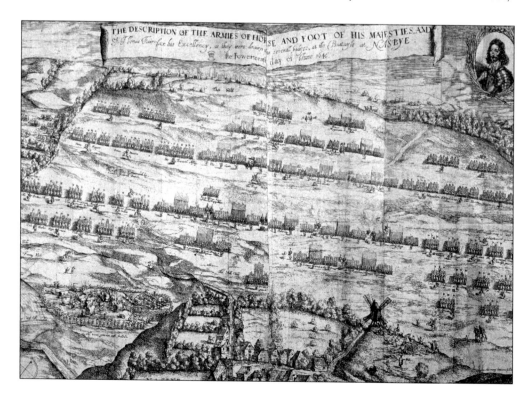

parliament drastically reorganised its war effort. A Self-Denying Ordinance was passed, under which almost all military commanders who were members of parliament had to lay down their commissions by spring 1645, thus removing most of the senior commanders of 1642–44, including Essex, the Earl of Manchester and Waller. In their place, a new batch of generally more dynamic and focused senior officers was appointed, including Sir Thomas Fairfax as lord general and overall commander-in-chief. At the same time, parliament grouped together several of its existing regional armies and brigades to create a large, national army under Fairfax's command. Called the New Model Army, it consisted of 12 foot regiments, 11 horse regiments and 10 companies of dragoons – around 22,000 men.

In late April 1645 Fairfax set out to relieve Taunton, while Cromwell harassed royalist outposts around Oxfordshire. On 7 May the king's main army left Oxford, heading first north towards Cheshire, but then swinging into the Midlands, storming and brutally sacking Leicester on 30 May. Fairfax, who from 19 May had been besieging Oxford, moved north to engage the king. Rendezvousing with further troops en route, by 13 June Fairfax had perhaps 15,000 men within a few miles of the king in Northamptonshire. Charles and his army of around 9–10,000 men turned to face them, occupying a ridge north of the village of Naseby overnight. In the early hours the parliamentarians occupied a similar and parallel ridge, closer to Naseby and a little under 1,000 yards from the royalist line. Battle began around 10 am on 14 June, when Rupert's horse on the royalist right charged forward, put the opposing cavalry to flight but then carried on galloping three miles or more from the battlefield in pursuit of the shattered parliamentary horse and the baggage train. The parliamentary infantry and its right wing of horse moved forward, and although the royalist infantry initially had the better of a close-quarter fight, Cromwell's horse on the right shattered

their greatly outnumbered opponents and then wheeled left to tear into the exposed flank of the royalist foot. Remnants of the parliamentary horse and dragoons on the left also rallied and began attacking the royalist foot. They buckled, broke and began surrendering, though some may have pulled back and attempted to make a last stand north of their original position. By early afternoon parliament had won a decisive victory and the king's army had been shattered beyond repair.

The civil war continued for another year as a grand mopping-up exercise, with parliamentary armies securing royalist territories and strongholds. Fairfax led most of the New Model Army to reconquer west and south-west England, wintering in Devon mid-way through this successful campaign. In the process, he inflicted further defeats over smaller royalist armies in battles at Langport on 10 July 1645, Bovey Tracey on 9 January 1646 and Torrington on 16 February 1646, captured Bridgwater on 23 July 1645, Bristol on 10 September 1645 and Exeter on 9 April 1646, and eventually accepted the surrender of Hopton and the remaining royalist troops near Truro on 10 March. Meanwhile the king's position in Wales and the Marches was collapsing. Parliamentary forces secured victories over regional royalist armies in small engagements at Colby Moor in Pembrokeshire on 1 August and outside Denbigh on 1 November, but most of Wales fell to parliament without a fight. The exception was a scattering of re-fortified Welsh castles, which often held out and withstood long and formal sieges before eventually surrendering on terms late in the war. In autumn 1645 the king tried to get help to his stronghold at Chester, one of very few large towns left in his hands, but a royalist army of relief was badly mauled in a running battle around Rowton Moor on 24 September and, after suffering several more months of close siege and bombardment, Chester surrendered on terms at the beginning of February. In autumn 1645 Cromwell led a detachment of the

New Model Army to mop up remaining royalist bases in southern England, capturing Devizes, Winchester and Basing House. On 21 March 1646 the last royalist field army of any note was overwhelmed at Stow-in-the-Wold. A few weeks later Charles himself slipped out of besieged Oxford and on 5 May he surrendered to the Scots besieging Newark. On his orders, most remaining royalist strongholds, including Newark and Oxford, surrendered, though a handful of outposts continued futile and pointless resistance and so endured close siege for a few more weeks or months.

The local war

Underlying these major campaigns was an intricate mosaic of local wars waged at county level. For example, there were repeated local campaigns and dramatically shifting fortunes in Pembrokeshire, the one part of Wales in which the parliamentarians were a real force and contested royalist dominance. Fighting began remarkably late in the day, for not until late summer 1643 did the royalist commander, the Earl of Carbery, attempt to impose his authority, securing the county's strongholds without serious resistance. Only

A contemporary image of Robert Devereux, Earl of Essex, lord general and commander-in-chief of the parliamentary armies from summer 1642 until he was forced to resign his commission in spring 1645 under the terms of the Self-Denying Ordinance. (Ann Ronan Picture Library)

Laugharne Castle was one of the few strongholds in Pembrokeshire which changed hands only after serious fighting. In late October 1644, as part of their reconquest of the county, the parliamentarians secured the town and then began a two-day bombardment of the castle and its royalist garrison. On 2 November they stormed the damaged gatehouse and outer ward of the castle, whereupon the royalists in the inner ward opened negotiations and surrendered the following day. The parliamentarians lost 10 men in the operation, the royalists over 30 dead. (Author's collection)

Pembroke resisted and stood out for parliament. Between autumn 1643 and spring 1644 it was reinforced by sea and in the opening months of 1644 served as a base from which parliamentarians quickly overran almost the whole county. The royalist hold was shown to be weak, the royalist commander was suspected of cowardice and the jumpy royalist garrison in Haverfordwest fled when movement was spotted on a nearby hill – a herd of black bullocks was mistaken for an advancing parliamentary army. But when a new, brutal royalist commander, Charles Gerrard, swept into Pembrokeshire with 2,000 men in summer 1644, he quickly recovered most of the county's strongholds, leaving the shaken parliamentarians penned up in Pembroke and Tenby. But at the end of August Gerrard and his army were called away to fight for the king in England, and the parliamentarians were able to regroup, venture forth and recapture most of the county in the closing months of 1644. The pattern was repeated in 1645, for Gerrard returned in the spring and mounted a whirlwind campaign which, by the end of May, had recovered almost the whole county and left the parliamentarians

shut up once more in Pembroke and Tenby. But at the end of May, Gerrard and most of his forces had left for England, this time never to return, and during the summer parliament's forces recovered control of the whole county. Although Pembroke had been in parliament's hands throughout and Tenby for most of the war, all the other strongholds of Pembrokeshire, its main towns and its dozen or more re-fortified castles, changed hands five times between the opening months of 1644 and the late summer of 1645. In Pembrokeshire the fortunes of the two parties fluctuated in a way that apparently had little to do with the ebb and flow of the national war. Isolated from the rest of the fighting by the buffer of solid and largely undisturbed royalist control of south and west Wales, Pembrokeshire endured its own, very distinctive local war, which seems semi-detached from the armed contest going on 100 miles (161km) or more away in England and the Welsh Marches.

No other county saw such remarkably swift and frequent changes of fortune, with six quickly alternating periods of royalist and parliamentary dominance. But the course of the fighting in many other counties followed distinctive courses. Different regions and counties clearly experienced very different types of war. The parliamentary heartlands – most territory east of a line from the Wash to the Channel near Littlehampton – were under parliament's control throughout and largely escaped direct fighting and bloodshed. Most of Wales (except Pembrokeshire), parts of the Marches and the far south-west of England were secured for the king with little opposition early in the war and remained firmly and peacefully under royalist control until 1645–46, when they fell to parliament fairly quickly and with only limited fighting. Other regions and counties were bitterly divided and hotly contested for long periods during the civil war and suffered intense fighting and bloodshed. Such areas included Gloucestershire, Yorkshire, Lincolnshire, the environs of Oxfordshire and large parts of the central, western and southern Midlands. It is noticeable that all five of the civil war battles of 1642–46 in which 25,000 or more troops fought – Edgehill, both battles of Newbury, Marston Moor and Naseby – as well as most of the seven or eight other battles involving more than 10,000 troops, took place in these areas. Other regions and counties come somewhere in the middle of this bloody league table.

Counties like Dorset and Somerset in the south, County Durham and Lancashire in the north, were divided, contested and garrisoned at times during the war, all changed hands at least once and all contained major strongholds which played a significant role. But with the exception of the one-sided encounter at Langport in Somerset late in the war, none saw a substantial field engagement during the first civil war and in every case much of the county was quiet and untroubled by fighting for much of war.

Substantial parts of England and Wales were not really contested during the civil wars. The moors of Cornwall, Devon and Somerset, the mountains of Wales and northern England, the uplands of the Pennine spine and Lancashire and Yorkshire, were of limited value during the war, for they were economically and materially poor and were sparsely populated. For the most part, these highland zones were neither garrisoned nor fought over. In Wales, garrisons and fighting were concentrated in the richer, more fertile and populous lowland zones, the coastal strips and the lush, rich farmlands and the prosperous towns and ports of Pembrokeshire. In Cumbria and Lancashire, action focused on controlling the main road running north–south through the region, from the Scottish border down to Cheshire, as well as the region's principal towns (many of them on or adjoining this road) such as Carlisle, Lancaster and Preston, and a string of re-fortified castles or manor houses overseeing either the main road or the richer, more fertile and populous lowland zone of Lancashire (the Fylde). Throughout the country, both sides concentrated their efforts and resources on securing, controlling or contesting rich and populous areas, key communication highways and intersections, the principal river valleys, centres of raw materials and production, ports and, above all, towns. Although England and Wales were not intensively urbanised in the 17th century, inland, riverine and coastal towns played a major role in the civil wars and, as centres of population, wealth, materials, markets, trade, manufacturing and communications, they were very valuable and often hotly contested.

Some towns were of regional or national importance during the war, including London as the nation's capital, Oxford after the king made it his headquarters and alternative capital, the port and regional capital of Bristol, the major military and maritime centres of Portsmouth and Hull, the king's northern capital of York, and Newark, massively fortified as a provincial royalist base. Gloucester and Chester came to attract the attention of major royalist or parliamentary armies. But scores of other towns were caught up in the fighting and became military centres in their own right, shaping the course of the war in that locality. The militarisation of a town might involve the repair of old medieval or Roman masonry walls and gates, the reinforcement of town walls by piling earth and turf against them to strengthen them against artillery, the construction of new lines of earthwork banks and ditches to enclose and defend the urban or suburban areas and the construction of self-contained outworks, earthwork forts and batteries to provide additional defensive firepower covering weak points or obvious lines of attack. In many cases, houses and suburbs outside the main defended area would be demolished by the defending troops in order to provide a clear area of sight and fire and to deny an approaching enemy any cover or vantage points for attack.

Above all, a garrison would be established – a base for a resident body of troops, anything from a few dozen to over 1,000-strong. The garrison's role was to cream off the resources of the town and its rural hinterland to supply the royalist or parliamentary war effort, to ensure that the town remained firmly under its control, to repulse any attempts by the enemy to disrupt that control or to plunder or capture the town, and to use the town as a base for raiding and attacking enemy garrisons, towns or other strongholds in the locality. A few towns served as military strongholds for one side even when most of the surrounding countryside was in the hands of its opponents. Chester held out as a royalist stronghold in a largely parliamentarian county, while Plymouth, Lyme Regis, Taunton, Gloucester, Pembroke and Hull were parliamentarian-held towns in royalist areas.

Garrisons and their activities also shaped and dominated the local war in rural areas. In the course of the war, hundreds of castles, manor houses and, in a few cases, churches in England and Wales were fortified or re-fortified to serve as military bases. Many medieval stone castles were semi-ruinous by the mid-17th century, but many could be re-roofed, re-floored, re-gated and thus made defensible quickly and easily. Again, in many cases outer earthworks were thrown up to strengthen the position. The role of a rural garrison was essentially the same as that of an urban garrison, though it might range more widely to pull in supplies and other resources. Indeed, most rural garrisons controlled a home patch, perhaps covering a number of surrounding parishes extending several miles, which they oversaw and from which they extracted further recruits, horses, money, food and drink, and a wide range of supplies. Their acquisitive ways often shaded into general plunder. Many garrisons ran what amounted to extortion or protection rackets, harassing the local civilian population, as much as mounting military operations against enemy units, patrols, garrisons and territory. The royalist Clarendon wrote that the king's garrison at Chipping Campden 'brought no other benefit to the public than the enriching the licentious governor thereof, who exercised an illimited tyranny over the whole country'. A few miles away, the Tudor mansion of Compton Wynyates in Warwickshire housed a parliamentary garrison in 1644–45 under the command of the abrasive George Purefoy. He ran a regime of terror, stealing and plundering almost indiscriminately, making heavy and repeated demands with menaces on the surrounding population, taking prodigious quantities of cash, hay, straw, oxen, horses, sheep, meat, crops, food and drink, utensils, furniture, fine clothes and bedding. He also kidnapped innocent civilian travellers on nearby roads, extracting payment for their release, and swooped down to plunder any valuables being transported through his patch. Purefoy's garrison and its actions

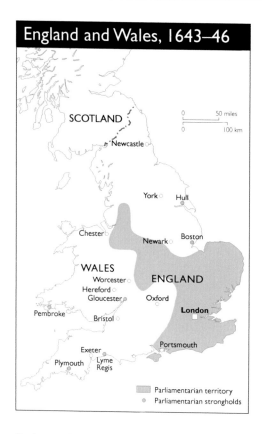

England and Wales, 1643–46

SCOTLAND

Newcastle

0   50 miles

0   100 km

York   Hull

Chester   Newark   Boston

WALES
Worcester   ENGLAND
Hereford
Gloucester   Oxford
Pembroke   London
Bristol

Portsmouth

Exeter
Plymouth   Lyme
Regis

Parliamentarian territory
Parliamentarian strongholds

Territory under parliamentary control from spring 1643 until the end of the war in summer 1646. As well as the parliamentary heartlands, naval dominance and control of the seas ensured that parliament also held throughout the war a string of major ports and coastal towns, such as Plymouth and Lyme Regis, Pembroke, Boston and Hull.

shaped and coloured the local war in large parts of Warwickshire and neighbouring north-west Oxfordshire during the closing two years of the war.

In most divided and contested areas, military action was dominated by local fighting, by the raiding and counter-raiding of local garrisons, by small battles and skirmishes fought by local armies and typically involving a few score or a few hundred rather than a few thousand on each side. As both sides sought to control and tie down territory, they committed a growing proportion of the total number of men in arms to garrison duty and to small local armies. As early as the Edgehill campaign, king and parliament were allocating men to

garrison duty and by 1644–45 probably both had nearly half their total manpower serving in garrisons and small, county-based units. Splitting their resources in this way represented something of a compromise, for the principal field armies and national campaigns were never as strong as they might have been, but a local military presence ensured that territory was controlled and its resources made available for a long war. Had it been possible to end the war in a single, huge field engagement, garrisoning the country in this way and maintaining a local war effort would have made no sense. But even by the time of Edgehill both sides were hedging their bets by looking to secure strongholds, and the inconclusive nature of that opening battle tended to confirm them in that policy.

In some areas, service in the local war, especially in a well-supplied and well-protected urban garrison, was quite pleasant and easy, preferable to fighting in a peripatetic field army. One newspaper described Newport Pagnell as a 'warm nest for a soldier in winter'. However, few strongholds were entirely safe – even Newport Pagnell suffered a surprise, night-time raid in summer 1645 that left a dozen or so dead – and many urban and rural garrisons in deeply divided and more fiercely contested regions suffered repeated raids and counter-raids. Small local forces, often drawn from garrisons, would sally out by day or night, clashing with other small enemy units in the open or swooping down on hopefully surprised and unprepared enemy strongholds. Even quite large and apparently well-fortified bases might fall to a surprise attack, such as Leeds, which fell to parliament in January 1643, and Shrewsbury, captured by parliament in a night attack on 22 February 1645. Alternatively, the stronghold might be subjected to a long and formal siege, in the hope that the enemy would eventually surrender through lack of food, the unpleasant and diseased conditions inside, the collapse of morale or the general hopelessness of their position. In the course of the war many towns, including Plymouth,

The Civil War in Wales, 1642–48

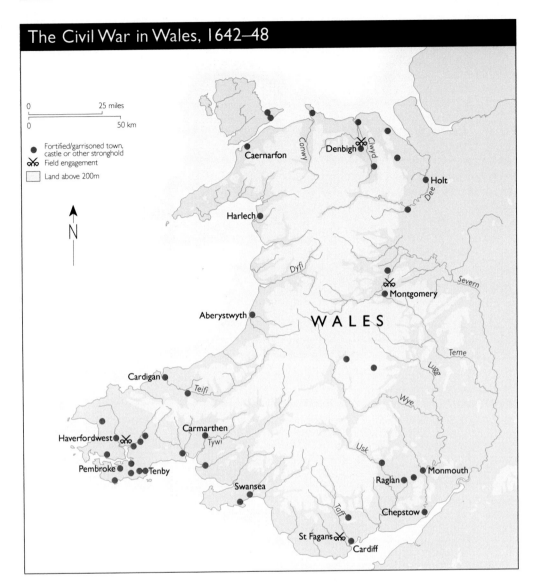

Exeter, Lyme Regis, Taunton, Bristol, Gloucester, Oxford, Portsmouth, Winchester, Reading, Newark, King's Lynn, Hull, Chester, York and a few other strongholds such as Lathom House, Basing House and Donnington Castle were subjected to quite lengthy, formal sieges by large or combined armies. There were scores of briefer or smaller siege operations during the conflict. The last phase of the war, in 1645–46, was dominated not by battles but by sieges, as parliamentary forces mopped up. The New Model Army alone undertook 46 sieges in the closing year or so of the war, and

The civil war in Wales. With very few exceptions, garrisons, fortified towns, other contested strongholds and the handful of field engagements fought within the principality were to be found in lowland areas, below 200 metres. The civil war in Wales, as in England, was predominantly a lowland, not a highland, conflict.

between the battle of Naseby in June 1645 and the surrender of the king's last mainland base, Harlech Castle, in March 1647, parliament captured over 80 royalist garrisons containing around 23,000 troops.

An attacking force could attempt to capture a garrison by first softening it up and

The late medieval castle at Raglan served as a major royalist base in south-east Wales throughout the civil war. During 1646 it was closely besieged and repeatedly bombarded by parliamentary forces and, after a 13-week siege, it eventually surrendered to Sir Thomas Fairfax on 19 August, one of the last bases on the mainland to do so. The buildings around the Pitched Stone Court (below) took the brunt of the parliamentary bombardment, and most of the windows and battlements were blown in. The apartments ranged around the inner courtyard, the Fountain Court (above), probably suffered less severely from the parliamentary bombardment, though the castle as a whole was rendered indefensible after the civil war and was abandoned. (Author's collection)

then storming and overwhelming the .
defenders. Softening up involved directing
heavy artillery at the defences in the hope of
opening a breach in the stone walls, or
lobbing explosive mortars over the defences
in the hope of causing death, destruction,
fear and fire within the stronghold. Once the
defences or defenders were deemed to be in a
much weakened position to resist, the hostile
force would assault the stronghold, pouring
in through gaping holes or carrying the
defences by scaling ladders, and hoping that
they would encounter limited resistance
once inside. The storming of a garrisoned
stronghold was often reckoned to be the
most terrifying and bloody aspect of the
local war. For example, in autumn 1644 local
parliamentarians stormed a royalist garrison
in the manor house at Abbotsbury in Dorset.
It turned into a desperate, six-hour fight,
though eventually the parliamentarians got
close enough to the main house to throw in
blazing furze and set the building ablaze.
Fire, smoke and heavy gunfire induced the
royalists to seek to surrender, but the
parliamentary commander ordered that
no quarter be given. Worse still, once the
parliamentarians had entered the burning
house to kill and plunder, a spark ignited the
royalist magazine and over 50 royalists and
parliamentarians perished in the explosion.
The overall death toll in this bloody though
ultimately successful operation was probably
over 100 and the Elizabethan mansion was
completely wrecked. A year later, in autumn
1645, Oliver Cromwell led part of the
New Model Army against Basing House in
Hampshire. The Marquis of Worcester's
massively fortified palace, comprising a
medieval and a Tudor house within very
strong earthwork, stone and brick defences,
had served as a major royalist outpost
throughout the war. Long a thorn in
parliament's side, it had resisted earlier sieges
and attacks, and Cromwell was determined
to end resistance once and for all. He arrived
with a large force and heavy artillery on
8 October and, once his summons had been
refused, his guns quickly opened up two
breaches in the outer defences. A little before

dawn on 14 October Cromwell stormed
Basing House, his 7,000-strong force quickly
overwhelming the 300 or so troops
defending the base, smashing their way in
and laying waste to the house in a brief and
bloody assault. Although quarter was at last
given to some of the garrison and to many
of the pro-royalist civilians who had taken
shelter in Basing, over 100 of the defenders
were killed – 'many of the Enemy our men
put to the sword, and some officers of
quality', Cromwell wrote later that day
– and around £200,000-worth of goods
were plundered. The house was reduced to
charred ruins, not only because of the
bombardment from Cromwell's artillery
but also through 'a fire which fell upon the
place since our taking of it' and it never
again served as either a military stronghold
or an elite residence.

Just as the local war dominated the
fighting in the English civil wars, so the
majority of military deaths occurred in these
contexts and in this type of warfare. It is
notoriously difficult for modern historians to
estimate the numbers of dead with precision
because contemporary accounts were often
vague or inconsistent and many of the
smaller actions, involving limited numbers of
combatants and fatalities, probably pass by
entirely unrecorded. However, the overall
pattern is clear. There were probably only
nine civil war battles fought in England and
Wales during the entire civil wars (including
the renewed fighting of 1648 and 1651) in
which more than 1,000 men were killed, and
it is likely that no more than 15 per cent of
the total number of military deaths in action
in England and Wales during 1642–51 were
sustained in major battles of this sort. It may
be that somewhere around 35–40,000 royalist
and around 30,000 parliamentary troops died
in action in England and Wales during the
first civil war of 1642–46, and of these the
great majority fell not in the major battles
and the principal national campaigns, but in
much smaller local and provincial actions. It
was during the dour fighting of the local,
territorial war, in the course of raids,
skirmishes, sieges and assaults on garrisons

There are numerous versions of this contemporary, three-quarter length portrait of Oliver Cromwell, by or after Robert Walker. This version, which hangs at Burghley House near Stamford in Lincolnshire, was reputedly given to the owner after Cromwell captured the house in the summer of 1643. In reality, this portrait, like most or all of the Walkers, probably dates from the late 1640s. (Bridgeman Art Library)

and in actions that often involved just a few score or at most a few hundred men, that the overwhelming majority of the military casualties occurred.

There is one other type of very specialised local war, the naval war. At the outbreak of the civil war, the navy declared for parliament and naval control remained with parliament throughout the war of 1642–46. The navy was able to undertake amphibious operations, landing reinforcements or supplies to relieve pressure on besieged coastal towns or bases and bombarding the royalist positions around the town. For example, in 1642 naval action helped secure or bolster parliament's hold over the key ports of Portsmouth and Hull and in 1643 it landed men and supplies to relieve the renewed royalist pressure on Hull. Naval supremacy and support explain why parliament was able to retain a string of key ports and coastal towns, such as Plymouth, Lyme Regis and Pembroke, even when they were surrounded on their landward side by a swathe of royalist territory. The navy also ensured that parliamentary troops, supplies and heavy artillery could be shipped from one port to another, often allowing far quicker and easier movement than could be achieved overland. Parliament's naval supremacy was also important in denying various opportunities to the king. Thus the royalists found it more difficult (though not impossible) to obtain supplies from the Continent, and parliament's Irish Sea guard proved very effective at thwarting attempts to ship royalist troops over from Ireland. There were limits to what the parliamentary navy could achieve, however, particularly if operating in an estuary or under sustained enemy fire. Thus in summer 1643 the navy was unable to give much aid to Exeter, which fell, or to Gloucester, which held out because of the dynamism of its garrison and the army of relief that marched across country. In summer 1644 the navy proved of little help to Essex and his army when they were trapped by the king between Lostwithiel and Fowey in Cornwall. Although parliamentary vessels tried to

prevent supplies reaching Chester, the naval blockade did little harm, and the royalist port and city finally fell only because of the actions of the besieging army and the collapse of royalist control over the neighbouring territory of north-east Wales. Perhaps one of the navy's greatest contributions to the parliamentary war effort was an indirect one, for by protecting merchant vessels using the port of London and by keeping open the principal water highways for trade and commerce, it ensured that the supplies themselves and the income accruing from customs duties paid on them continued to flow to parliament.

To live and die a soldier

In the summers of 1643, 1644 and 1645 there were up to 150,000 men in arms in England and Wales and several hundred thousand served as soldiers at some stage of the war. From 1643 onwards both sides resorted to conscription, repeatedly requiring county administrators to impress men. They had to be reasonably fit adults – it was not acceptable to draft children, the elderly, the ill or the deformed, and both clergy and gentlemen's sons were usually exempt. Those viewed as idle, trouble-makers, petty criminals, vagrants, the unemployed or unemployable were scooped up first, followed by others whose loss would not hurt families or communities too much, such as. bachelors and younger sons. Many resisted conscription, hated army life and deserted at the first opportunity. 'They longed for nothing more than to see their own Chimneys,' Waller wrote of the hundreds who deserted his army in summer 1644. All armies suffered from desertion, which was endemic and impossible to prevent, despite half-hearted and intermittent attempts to locate and round up deserters.

Volunteer or conscript, a soldier should have had all his immediate needs met by the army. He was to be provided with a set of clothes and a pair of shoes or boots, arms and

NATHANIEL FINES .
MIREVELT. PINX.

Nathaniel Fiennes took up arms for parliament in summer 1642, fought at Edgehill and was appointed governor of Bristol in spring 1643 . He was accused of cowardice and treachery after he surrendered Bristol to the royalists in late July 1643 and in December he was tried and found guilty of improperly surrendering the town and sentenced to death, though promptly reprieved. His military career over, he probably spent the next few years abroad, but his political career resumed in the late 1640s and he became an important and powerful figure in the 1650s, during the Protectorate of Oliver Cromwell. (Lord Saye, Broughton Castle, Banbury, Oxfordshire)

armour appropriate to his rank and role, a daily food ration which typically included bread, cheese, meat, grains or pulses and beer, and a weekly wage, ranging from around 5s a week in the infantry to 12s 6d in the dragoons and 17s 6d in the cavalry, though the latter had to feed their mounts at their own expense. In practice, all these necessities were often in short supply and civil war

soldiers had to make good the shortfall. The dead and the captured would routinely be stripped of clothing, footwear, arms and armour, and soldiers would live off the land, undertaking a mixture of foraging, rustling, plundering and plain theft in search of food, money or goods to sell for hard cash. There are plenty of contemporary accounts of troops going hungry and of famished soldiers

The late medieval, moated castle of Nunney in Somerset housed a royalist garrison from 1643 until 1645. After a two month siege and bombardment, the king's men eventually surrendered on 20 August 1645. (Author's collection)

breaking off a fight on chancing upon a store of food or alcohol. For example, a parliamentary attack on Basing House failed in part because the troops captured a barn full of provisions and stopped to eat and drink their fill, even though they were under heavy fire and the barn's roof was ablaze. Essex's soldiers soon polished off the 2,500 royal deer in Windsor Great Park.

Soldiers serving in the principal field armies generally moved around the country a great deal. Major armies were typically on the move one day in two during the campaigning season, marching perhaps eight or ten miles a day and covering hundreds of miles in a season. New sights and sounds confronted them – Londoners allegedly in wonder at the sight of cows and running after them to take a closer look, the people of the Cotswolds bemused by the strange accents of troops from Hackney and Tower Hamlets in their midst, Captain Richard Symonds rushing off to visit and sketch local churches wherever the king's army halted. But the overwhelming image from contemporary sources is of the misery of military life: the cold, fear, hunger and tiredness which it engendered. Soldiers' accounts are littered with tales of woe: 'our regiment stood in the open field all night, having neither bread nor water to refresh ourselves, having also marched the day before without any sustenance, neither durst we kindle any fire, though it was a very cold night', and 'cold lodging without any refreshment, for the souldiers could not the day before, in all their hard march, get any considerable modicum of bread and beere ... we lay all in the open field, upon the plowd-land, without straw, having neither bread nor water.' A lucky few might be billeted in civilian households and provided with a decent meal and a warm bed, but for ordinary soldiers on the move barns, sheds or bare earth generally awaited them at the end of the day. Considering that the summers of the 1640s were amongst the coolest and wettest of the 17th century, it is small wonder that so many soldiers succumbed to disease.

Sir Ralph Hopton summarised his approach to command as 'pay well, command well, hang well'. Both sides generally respected the rights of captured enemy troops and mutual restraint was exercised. Prisoners might be stripped,

roughly treated and transported to various murky castles, but with the exception of a few turncoats deemed to have betrayed their trust, most captured troops were not executed. In 1644 parliament did initiate a policy of immediately executing any captured royalists thought to have come from Ireland, but when Rupert and others responded by executing matching numbers of parliamentary prisoners, this policy was pursued with much less vigour, though not entirely abandoned. Instead military executions, generally by hanging, were mainly used to impose discipline within an army. From time to time, a few unfortunate deserters or plunderers might be strung up as an example, but soldiers were more likely to be hanged for mutiny, rape, killing a military colleague or murdering an innocent, non-combatant civilian. A few officers faced the noose or the firing squad, especially those deemed to have surrendered a stronghold prematurely or without good cause. Thus the parliamentarians shot Thomas Steele for surrendering Beeston Castle in December 1643 and the royalists Francis Windebanke for surrendering Blechingdon House in April 1645. In 1643 the royalist governor of Reading and the parliamentary governor of Bristol were condemned for surrendering those towns, but both were reprieved.

Siege operations brought their own horrors. In a prolonged siege, living conditions deteriorated, food ran short and disease was rife. During the siege of Scarborough Castle in summer 1645 over half the royalist garrison died, many from scurvy and malnutrition. The remainder became too weak to bury the dead, and when they finally surrendered most of the surviving troops were unable to walk. During a prolonged siege in 1645 the royalist defenders of Nunney Castle reputedly tortured the one live pig they had left, hoping that its loud squealing would convince the besieging force that the garrison had many animals and so plenty of food and would abandon the operation. When the royalists finally surrendered

St Bertoline's church in Barthomley, Cheshire, was the scene of one of the most notorious massacres of the civil war, when in December 1643 royalist troops murdered a group of unarmed civilians within the church. Over a decade later retribution was exacted, for in October 1654 the royalist officer in charge at Barthomley, Major John Connaught, was tried for murder at the Chester assizes, convicted and duly hanged for his crime. (Author's collection)

Beeston Castle in November 1645 all they had left was a piece of turkey pie, two biscuits, one live peacock and a peahen.

Attempts to storm rather than starve out a besieged stronghold were amongst the bloodiest operations of the entire war. At one point in the unsuccessful royalist attacks on Lyme Regis 'so many were slain that the water that served the town was coloured with Blood', and when Preston was successfully stormed in 1643 'Nothing was heard but "Kill dead!" "Kill dead!" was the word in the town, killing all before them without any respect ... their horse men pursuing the poor amazed people, killing, stripping and spoiling all they could meet with.' According to one estimate, over 20,000 direct military deaths, or roughly a quarter of all the deaths in action in England and Wales during the civil wars, occurred in sieges.

At times, the slaughter might be so extensive and indiscriminate that it shaded into massacre or atrocity. The royalists, Rupert especially, gained an unfortunate reputation for storming towns with great brutality and unleashing killing and plunder. The royalist storming and sacking of Brentford in autumn 1642, Birmingham in 1643, during which the royalists reportedly 'hacked, hewed and pistolled all they met with', and Bolton in 1644 became notorious. On a handful of occasions the killing was more premeditated. Thus in March 1644, when the royalists stormed and captured a small garrison at Hopton Castle, Shropshire, the defenders were stripped and tied back to back, their throats were slit and their bodies tossed into a ditch. At other times, troops turned on civilians. At Christmas 1643 a royalist army out of Chester, reinforced from Ireland, attacked a group of local inhabitants who had sought refuge in Barthomley church, smoking out several who were cowering in the tower. The royalists then stripped and attacked their civilian prisoners, cutting the throats of some, stabbing and axing others, killing 12 on the spot. One royalist crowed that 'I put them all to the sword; which I find to be the best way

to proceed with these kind of people, for mercy to them is cruelty'.

Battle brought other horrors. 'You cannot imagine what hot service it is,' wrote one officer after his first engagement. Artillery and musket fire caused deafening blasts and spread thick, acrid smoke across the battlefield. One parliamentary captain compared Marston Moor to 'Hell's gates', writing that the infantry 'made such a noise with shot and clamour of shouts that we lost our ears, and the smoke of powder was so thick that we saw no light, but what proceeded from the mouth of the guns'. The

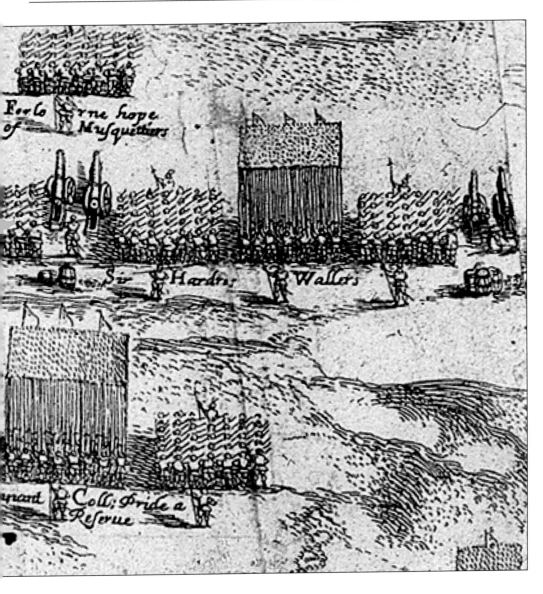

The labels within the image read:
Forlo of — Hope Musquetiers.
Sir Hardn. Wallers
reard Coll: Pride a Reserue

smoke at Naseby was so thick, one officer recalled, that 'the foot on either side hardly saw each other until they were within Carbine shot'. Given the problems of smoke and the general confusion of a battle, contemporaries were well aware that no single participant would later be able to give a clear account of the engagement as a whole. As the infantry bunched and fought together in packs, each man had limited freedom of movement and field of vision. Many historians have likened close-quarter infantry combat to encounters between rival football crowds thickly packed on the

This enlargement from part of Streeter's plan of Naseby depicts the parliamentary infantry deployed at the start of the battle, with alternating blocks of pikemen and musketeers quite tightly packed together. So long as these units maintained their cohesion in battle, the army could continue to fight and casualties would generally be quite modest. (Heritage Image Partnership)

terraces, with blocks of men pushing forward and those at the interface prodding and lashing out at each other, in this case with pikes, swords or the butt end of muskets. Elsewhere on the battlefield, rival cavalry might be exchanging pistol shot or engaging at close quarters with their broad swords. So long as infantry and cavalry units held together and maintained their cohesion, the army could continue the fight and casualties would generally be modest. But when units began breaking and turning in flight, the army as a whole started collapsing and the bloodletting of a rout would begin. Defeated cavalry could spur on their horses and stand a fair chance of getting away, but fleeing infantry could be cut down almost at will by the victorious cavalry. After one victory, a royalist claimed that the king's horse had pursued the fleeing foot 'until their swords were blunted with the slaughter', and a parliamentarian wrote of the royalist infantry fleeing from Marston Moor: 'We had cleared the field of all enemies, and followed the chase of them ... cutting them down so that their dead bodies lay three miles in length.'

Civil war soldiers died in large numbers from contagious diseases, many of which went under the general heading 'camp fever'. Living close together in poor conditions encouraged and spread disease in armies and garrisons. Accidents on and off the battlefield – guns going off inadvertently or exploding when faulty, gunpowder ignited by stray sparks or careless handing, broken necks caused by falls from horses, drownings from falling into rivers or being swept away while attempting to ford them – accounted for other deaths. Fatalities in the major battles, the smaller engagements and skirmishes and the siege operations of the civil war probably amounted to somewhere around 75,000 deaths in England and Wales in 1642–46. If they were not too deep and neither sepsis nor gangrene had set in, stabbing and slashing wounds from sword and pike might not be fatal. Burns and broken bones, too, might heal. But a

musket ball caused so much internal damage and, if it went through the body, such a huge exit wound, that many hits were fatal. Soldiers struck by cannon balls usually died. No soldier in the civil war was immune from death in action: at times Charles and Essex were exposed to fire or saw those close by them shot down; Fairfax, Cromwell, Hopton and many other generals were wounded and an array of aristocrats, including Lindsey, Northampton, Denbigh, Brooke and Falkland, died in action.

The various ways in which ordinary soldiers might perish are revealed in Richard Gough's account of the deaths of 13 of the 20 local men from Myddle and two neighbouring villages in north Shropshire who had volunteered to fight for the king in 1642. Six never returned and were presumed dead; one had been reported killed in action, though Gough did not know where; one died in action at Oswestry; one, a notorious plunderer, was wounded by his colleagues in an alehouse brawl near Bridgnorth and, unable to move, was burned to death when much of the town was fired in the course of a parliamentary attack; two perished in the massacre at Hopton Castle (so by 1644 they must, in fact, have been serving in the parliamentary garrison); and a father and son died while serving in the High Ercall garrison, the father expiring (perhaps of natural causes) in his bed, his son executed for stealing horses. Of the handful of local men who had volunteered for parliament, Gough knew of none killed, though one had his femur broken by a musket ball and his leg 'was very crooked as long as he lived'. As Gough concluded, 'if so many died out of these three towns, we may reasonably guess that many thousands died in England in that war.'

Soldiers' stories

Nehemiah Wharton

The series of letters which the London apprentice Nehemiah Wharton wrote as he marched off with the parliamentary army in summer 1642 are doubly valuable. Firstly, although like all military accounts written by combatants in the war, this source is socially skewed, coming from the literate upper levels of society, Wharton was less elevated than most, from the urban artisan class rather than the rural landed elite. Secondly, they throw light upon the opening weeks of the conflict, covering the period from mid-August onwards. Sergeant Wharton's letters are dominated by an ostensibly mundane round of marching, scavaging and minor skirmishing as he and his fellow soldiers marched from London to Worcester via Coventry and Northampton. He was not present at the battle of Powick Bridge – though he was anxious to discover accurate details of the engagement – and the series of letters closes on 7 October, well before Edgehill. But they are full of the fascinating minutiae of the opening phase of the war, as troops got used to the hardship of military life, of foraging for food and drink – Wharton acquired a taste for poached venison as well as strong beer, including a barrel of 'ould Hum' – and of 'long and tedious' marches and the strain of sentry duty. His letters are littered with references to 'foule weather', noting on one occasion that 'before I marched one mile I was wet to the skin', on another that he was 'up to the ancles in thick clay'. Marching to Hereford in early October, he and his men were assailed by 'rain and snow, and extremity of cold', which killed one of them. On several occasions he failed to get a billet at the end of the day and spent the night with his men in the open air, picking and eating any

available fruit, huddled around fires made from hedges and uprooted fences and gates, singing psalms through the night. Wharton was 'exceeding sick' on one occasion, but soon recovered. He saw the dead and the dying en route, a royalist drummer with his arm shot off and another dead drummer by 'our knapsack boyes rifled to the shirt, which was very louzy', and he helped bury 28 corpses found when they entered Worcester. He reported several fatal accidents, fellow soldiers or civilian bystanders killed when muskets went off accidentally, as well as the rough treatment of a prostitute who had followed the troops to Coventry – she was paraded, pilloried, caged and ducked in the river. On a happier note, in Coventry Wharton had a winter suit made up, trimmed with gold and silver lace.

Two broader traits emerge from Wharton's letters. Firstly, he and many of his colleagues were motivated by a strong godly or puritan zeal. Uplifted by several 'famous', 'worthy' or 'heavenly' sermons preached to the troops, they seized the opportunity to attack their religious opponents. Joint pressure secured the removal of their lieutenant-colonel, who was felt to be ungodly. 'Papist' gentlemen were routinely threatened and plundered en route, relieved of food, drink and game, though senior officers tried to curb this activity. Particularly in the opening fortnight of the march, a string of parish churches were visited and purified by removing Arminian elements. Prayer books and surplices were destroyed, painted windows smashed, altar rails ripped out and burnt. Wharton reported how a group of soldiers used plundered surplices, hoods and caps to dress up as the Archbishop of Canterbury. He was shocked to see shops open and people at work in Worcester on a Sunday and berated the ignorant townsmen. Secondly, Wharton was in wonder at the various sites he visited and anxious to record what he saw, 'the passages of my pilgrimage' as he put it. Thus Buckinghamshire was 'the sweetest country that ever I saw'. Although he did not have time to visit Warwick itself, he saw and noted its hilltop castle as he marched by and did explore the surrounding countryside, seeing chapels, springs and gardens. He was very impressed with the streets, houses, churches and walls of Coventry, which he felt compared favourably with London, though he found Northampton in many ways more impressive still. Worcestershire clearly delighted Wharton, who became quite lyrical about the 'pleasaunt, fruitfull, and rich countrey, aboundinge in corne, woods, pastures, hills and valleys, every hedge and heigh way beset with fruits', especially pears 'whereof they make that pleasant drinke called perry', which was better than anything he had tasted in London. Although he thought the townspeople godless and popish, he liked Worcester itself, describing its walls, gates and bridge and its 'very stately cathederal' – the tombs of King John and Prince Arthur had particularly caught his eye – and was anxious to view and sketch the earthwork defences being thrown up around the town. Twice he rode to Malvern and, 'after much toyle', climbed the hills above the town to take in the view, which on a clear day Wharton reckoned extended 'neare thirty miles round'.

Richard Atkyns

Richard Atkyns was a country gentleman from Gloucestershire, in his late 20s at the time of the war. Early in 1643 he accepted an invitation to be a captain in a cavalry regiment being raised for the king and for around six months, between March and September 1643, he campaigned in southern England under Prince Maurice. He left a brief account of his fairly short military career within his much longer *Vindication*, written and published in the late 1660s. As a

retrospective account, written a quarter of a century later, it lacks some of the breathless immediacy of Wharton's letters and also contains a few factual errors, though Atkyns's memory was generally good and his account often colourful and vivid. His first action was a scrappy fight with Waller's parliamentarians at Little Dean in Gloucestershire on 11 April. His horse gave way, perhaps reduced by the sight and sounds of battle to hopeless 'trembling and quaking', but on a borrowed mount Atkyns was one of a dozen or so junior officers who charged a body of parliamentary musketeers; they turned and fled without firing a shot. However, in over-exuberant pursuit, Atkyns and his colleagues fell into a parliamentary ambush and he was lucky to escape – his buff coat was slashed by enemy swords and a musket ball fired by one of his colleagues took off a bar of his helmet and 'went through my hair' but 'did me no hurt'. Later in April, he was present at the unsuccessful royalist attempt to relieve besieged Reading, horrified at the sight of crack royalist troops, ordered to attack a strongly defended parliamentary position, dropping 'like ripe fruit in a strong wind' in the face of withering musket fire. On the evening of 10 June, in the course of a skirmish around Chewton Mendip in Somerset, Atkyns played a prominent role in a counter-attack which rescued Prince Maurice, who had been wounded and briefly captured by Waller's men. In the evening gloom and mist, Atkyns's groom lent Maurice his horse to make good his escape and was richly rewarded by the prince. Atkyns next encountered this fellow 15 years later, 'begging in the streets of London, with a muffler before his face, and spoke inwardly, as if he had been eaten up with the foul disease', a fate which probably befell many damaged and unemployed veterans.

The high-points of Atkyns's account are probably his descriptions of the battles of Lansdown and Rounday Down in July. Atkyns provides vivid descriptions not only of the bitter, dour struggle at Lansdown, 'the air so darkened by the smoke of the powder that…there was no light seen, but what the fire of the volleys of shot gave', but also of the catastrophic explosion of an ammunition cart after the battle, caused by parliamentary prisoners careless with a match given them to light their tobacco. Atkyns, who was near the cart at the time, apparently escaped unscathed, though he noted the deafening noise, the darkening of the air and the 'lamentable screeches' of the survivors, many of them 'miserably burnt'. Falling back on Oxford after the battle, Atkyns was so tired that he fell asleep leaning on a post while his horse was reshod, fell off his horse repeatedly thereafter and, reeling as if drunk, eventually reached the house of a relative and slept for 14 hours. In his description of Roundway Down, he gives a superb account of the difficulty of harming a cuirassier, for no matter how he slashed at Sir Arthur Heselrige with his sword or discharged pistols at point blank range against his helmet, Heselrige's armour was impregnable.

Eventually surrounded by other royalists and with his horse repeatedly stabbed and giving way beneath him, Heselrige agreed to surrender, but at that point he was rescued by parliamentary colleagues and Atkyns was forced away. The sudden departure of his groom, a 'rogue', taking with him Atkyns's spare clothes and other belongings, left him for a time without a change of clothes, and he was forced to go around in dirty and blood-stained clothes so that 'I became so lousy in three or four days, that I could not tell what to do with myself'. When he eventually procured a change of clothes, the old ones were so rotten through blood and sweat that they fell off him in tatters. Thereafter Atkyns's account trails off. He was present at the capture of Bristol in late July, but gives a rather brief and colourless description and, soon after, apparently thinking that the king's cause was safe and overall royalist victory assured, he left the army, never to return.

The wider context

Administration in wartime

Overall control of parliament's war effort and the wartime government and administration of territory in parliament's hands lay with the Long Parliament, sitting in more or less permanent session at Westminster. It claimed total legislative powers, and draft legislation that passed both Houses was issued as ordinances with full statutory power even though they did not have the royal assent. Parliament passed a string of ordinances to create field armies, appoint military commanders and establish and empower regional and local administrative machines. Both Houses were much depleted, for many peers and MPs had left London either to slip into quiet neutrality at home or abroad or to join the king at Oxford and actively support the royalist side. For much of the period 1642–46 around 30 peers sat in the Lords and around 200 MPs in the Commons. Towards the end of the war, the sitting MPs began permanently excluding absent colleagues and authorising a string of by-elections to fill vacancies. From the outset, parliament also set up a powerful central council to take on some of the administrative and executive burdens, comprising in the main MPs and peers, but also including a few non-members. This body was generally called the Committee of Safety down to the end of 1643, when it was enlarged to include some Scots representing parliament's new ally and was re-dubbed the Committee of Both Kingdoms. It met almost daily at the height of the war, generally at Derby House in Whitehall. Between them, parliament and council oversaw the war effort, liaised with the parliamentary commander-in-chief and other leading generals and co-ordinated the work of provincial and county administrative bodies.

The king and immediate entourage, generally based at his wartime capital of Oxford but peripatetic while Charles was campaigning, provided political and administrative leadership on the royalist side. The Privy Council continued to exist, but Charles quickly saw the need for a smaller, more select body of political and military advisers, and he established a powerful Council of War to support the war effort. Many members of the Long Parliament had joined the king at Oxford, and in 1643 he decided to set up a rival parliament there. Although the active membership of its two Houses was not far short of the numbers sitting in London, its work was far more limited, dressing up royal proclamations and declarations in a veneer of legislative normality. Even this propaganda role dwindled and the royalist parliament was wound up in 1645, as Oxford itself came under increasing pressure.

Both sides sought to establish provincial administrations, generally under the command of a senior peer, to pool the military and material resources of clusters of neighbouring counties and to co-ordinate military action within the region. Some of these regional administrations proved quite effective. For example, parliament's Eastern Association, comprising Essex, Hertfordshire, Suffolk, Norfolk and Cambridgeshire, with Huntingdonshire and Lincolnshire added later, pulled together and its regional army, commanded first by Lord Grey and then by the Earl of Manchester, played an important defensive and offensive role within its home patch and beyond until it was absorbed into the New Model Army in spring 1645. But many parliamentary and royalist provincial units worked less well, either because the overall commander lacked drive, dynamism and strong administrative support or because the territory lacked cohesion and fell prey to the particularism of individual counties.

Most wartime administration was conducted at the county level, and county-based administrative bodies supplied and supported the war effort and enabled both sides to mount and wage such a long and intense civil war. In 1642–43, as territory was carved up and king and parliament gained control over different parts of England and Wales, each established a string of committees to run the counties. A county committee generally numbered between a dozen and 40 members, drawn from the top levels of society, the landed elite, though in some counties members of the lesser gentry, mere gentlemen and esquires rather than knights, baronets and peers, acquired a more prominent role than they would normally have attained in peacetime. County committees often met several times a week, some always in the main or county town, some deliberately visiting different parts of the county. Where records survive, they consistently show that the workload was distributed unevenly, for many members rarely attended, leaving an inner core of strongly committed and highly active members to drive the work forward. Indeed, in some counties, particularly on the parliamentary side, the administration came to be dominated by a single figure, a county boss such as Sir William Brereton in Cheshire, Sir Anthony Weldon in Kent, Herbert Morley and Anthony Stapley jointly in Sussex. In addition to the principal county committee, there were often sub-committees or other specialist bodies, with overlapping membership, to help carry the workload.

This was important, for the county committee's workload was enormous. In most areas the principal means of local justice and administration, the magistrates' quarter and petty sessions, ceased during wartime and their functions effectively passed to the county committee, many of whose members were JPs. Thus the work of punishing local petty criminals (often by conscripting them), regulating alehouses, organising poor relief

and overseeing repairs to bridges and highways fell to the county committee. But its main work was geared directly to supporting the war effort. It had to find and provide the men, horses, food and drink, clothing and other materials for local and national armies and garrisons. Above all, it had to raise enormous sums to wage a massively expensive war. A foot regiment cost around £15,000 per year and a horse regiment around £30,000 per year; even a fairly small garrison cost £5–10,000 per year; a major operation, such as the siege of Chester, could cost £5,000 per week; the Eastern Association's army cost around £35,000 per month; and the parliamentary navy cost up to £500,000 per year. The total, direct military cost of the civil war is impossible to calculate, but historians estimate that it fell somewhere within the range £5–10 million, and was probably closer to the upper than the lower figure. Almost all the money raised to fund the war was imposed and collected at the county level; much of it never physically passed through a central treasury but was disbursed at the local level. Finance thus dominated the work of the county committees.

Via their county committees, both sides adopted remarkably similar policies for raising money. In summer 1642, in the hope and expectation of a short war and quick victory, both sides had looked to voluntary gifts or loans, in cash or plate, from their wealthier supporters. As the war continued and intensified, both sides applied more pressure, going back to the early contributors and seeking further donations, but also encouraging or compelling payment from the wealthier members of society who had not hitherto made voluntary contributions. Thus early in 1643 parliament empowered its county committees to extract set amounts, based on one-fifth of yearly income and/or one-twentieth of the value of an estate, from anyone with an income or estate above set thresholds who had not come forward in 1642 and given to the voluntary collection known as 'the Propositions'.

From 1643 both sides also began seizing part or all of those enemy estates that lay within their territories. Royalists sequestrated the estates of known parliamentarians or neutrals, parliamentarians those of royalists, neutrals or Catholics. The confiscated land might be run directly by the sequestrators and a steady income creamed off, but more often than not it was rented out or sold off. Very often, particularly towards the end of the war as the parliamentarians gained control, royalists and neutrals might recover part or all of their own estates by 'compounding for their delinquency', that is, paying a substantial fine to parliament.

From 1643, too, both sides began trying to impose excise duties on various goods. This was an unpopular tax and difficult to impose and collect in wartime, though it became a major source of income once the war had ended. Above all, from 1643–44 both sides imposed a direct tax, payable on all forms of income, which was collected weekly, fortnightly or monthly and to which all but the poorest members of communities would have been liable. The royalists called this tax the contribution, parliament the assessments. They imposed a very heavy burden, probably the equivalent of a direct tax of 10–12 per cent, were collected very effectively – parliamentary records suggest that even in wartime over 90 per cent of the money due on assessments was actually collected – and raised huge sums of money. By late 1643 parliament was levying over £35,000 per week from its territories. A county like Warwickshire was assessed for over £30,000 per year for much of the war, many counties found themselves paying considerably more in assessments each month than they had paid in ship money per year during the 1630s, and in 1644 the treasurer of the Eastern Association was receiving income equivalent to the pre-war annual income of the crown. Records suggest that even small villages far removed from the fighting paid out well over £1,000 in assessments over the period 1643–46.

Sadly, we know little about the work of many royalist county committees, for many of the administrative records of the losing side have apparently perished. In contrast, there are fairly full records for many counties administered by parliamentary committees during the war. They are dominated by financial accounts, enabling historians to reconstruct the financing of the local and national war effort on the parliamentary side. Between 1643 and the end of 1646, something approaching £200,000 was raised for parliament in Cheshire. Sequestrated property contributed almost half this sum (an unusually large proportion of the total income), while assessments contributed around £35,000 (an unusually small proportion). The voluntary Propositions and enforced exactions on those who had not contributed brought in around £35,000, the excise a fairly modest £10,000 and a variety of purely local taxes and levies another £30,000. Cheshire was not a particularly large, populous or prosperous county and, until the surrender of Chester in February 1646, its major town, port and commercial centre lay beyond the reach of parliamentary tax collectors. Kent, a larger and more prosperous county, all of which was in parliament's hands throughout the war, brought in a lot more money, perhaps up to £750,000 in total between 1642 and 1646. Over and above these neat figures, we must also remember the hidden or indirect costs of war in every county, the seizure of cash, goods and property by soldiers, the enforced free billeting, the crops taken or trampled underfoot by armies, the destruction of houses and so on, which in many areas probably equalled or exceeded the sums raised by taxes. The surviving accounts also confirm that almost all the money raised, typically 90 per cent or more of it, was spent on the war, financing local, regional and national armies, supporting the county's garrisons, and buying arms and ammunition, clothes and horses which were then sent off for military use. The civil war was an enormously expensive operation.

Civilians in wartime

Civilians could be directly caught up in the fighting in a number of ways. They could be drafted into the army, for both sides employed conscription extensively from 1643 onwards. They might find themselves caught in the middle of a minor skirmish, in the way or within range of stray shots when a raiding party smashed into a village or ran into enemy troops. A few civilians were attached to the main field armies, including wagoners and attendants and an assortment of wives, mistresses and prostitutes, and they might come under attack in the aftermath of a major field engagement as the victorious army plundered the baggage train. For example, after Naseby the parliamentarians attacked and disfigured or killed a group of women accompanying the royalist baggage train, mistaking the Welsh wives and girlfriends of some of the royalist troops for Irish Catholics. Civilians could not avoid being caught up in the war when a field army marched by or when their town, village or local stronghold was garrisoned, for many householders were required to feed and billet troops. John Hacket was one of tens of thousands who must have been hurt and aggrieved to be eaten out of house and home in this way, complaining, 'We call it free quarter. What a grief! to be made servile to provide for such guests, ... what an expense it was to bring out all the stores, laid up for a year, and to waste it in a week.'

Far worse was the experience of civilians living in a garrisoned town or village which

This enlargement from part of Streeter's plan of Naseby shows civilians, presumably locals, gathered on a vantage point close to Naseby windmill to watch the unfolding battle. Innocent or inquisitive bystanders could on occasion find themselves caught up in the action, in range of charging troops or stray shots. (Heritage Image Partnership)

was besieged, attacked or stormed. The civilians suffered along with the troops from the lack of food and water and from the effects of disease and bombardment by cannon and mortar. Moreover, an opposing army who managed to breach the defences and came storming in, its blood up, rampaging through the streets, was often not too worried about whether it was shooting and hacking down members of the garrison or civilians who were in the wrong place at the wrong time. For example, there were repeated allegations that when the royalists stormed Birmingham in 1643, Bolton in 1644

and Leicester in 1645, large numbers of the townspeople perished. Where they escaped with their lives, civilians in a town that had changed hands would generally not emerge materially and financially unscathed. For example, 75 inhabitants of Montgomery, from the bailiff and rector down to ordinary shopkeepers and householders, claimed damage and loss of property totalling £3,000 (an average of over £40 a head) when the town was captured by parliament and briefly retaken by the royalists in September 1644. Although doubtless exaggerated, these figures give an indication of the sort of damage that

could be inflicted in just a few days when rival armies vied for control of a town. And even those civilians in town and countryside who managed to avoid the main fighting or were lucky enough to live in a region that was not hotly contested were, without exception, vulnerable to plunder, extortion and plain robbery with menaces at the hands of the soldiers, and were liable to be imprisoned or killed outright if they resisted. Thus Bulstrode Whitelocke recalled that when royalist troops descended on his country seat, they consumed £200-worth of hay and corn, 'littered their horses with sheaves of good

wheat and gave them all sorts of corn', tore up many of Whitelocke's books in his study, using pages 'to light their tobacco', and carried other books away with them, presumably to sell. All this plunder and mayhem was on top of the unprecedented burden of heavy and repeated taxation extracted from the civilian population to finance the war effort.

While some civilians were killed in battles, skirmishes, sieges and stormings or in foolishly trying to resist plundering troops, far more died through catching the various diseases carried by the troops. Just as the unhealthy lifestyles and cramped conditions of many armies and garrisons encouraged and spread contagious illnesses, so the military presence alongside the civilian population enabled those diseases to spread amongst non-combatants. From the surviving records it is generally impossible to distinguish reliably between civilian and military deaths. We cannot be sure, for example, how many of the 3,000 or so who died in Plymouth during the prolonged civil war blockade and siege were members of the parliamentary garrison and how many were ordinary townspeople. But it has been estimated that on top of the 80,000 or more direct military deaths (i.e. deaths in action in England and Wales during the civil wars), there were up to 100,000 additional deaths over and above the normal level of peacetime mortality, caused by disease. A significant though unquantifiable proportion of those killed by military-borne disease would have been civilians.

The civil war also divided families, turning father against son and brother against brother. Amongst the landed elite these divisions are fairly easy to trace and are well documented. Although head counts and

A view from the hill upon which the castle stands across the town of Montgomery. During September 1644 the lightly defended town changed hands three times, in the course of which the townspeople alleged losses totalling around £3,000 through burning or other damage to their houses and through the seizure of cash, personal and household goods, crops, cattle and food by parliamentary and royalist troops. (Author's collection)

estimates vary, several historians have suggested that overall somewhere around 15 per cent of the elite landed families who took up arms in the civil war were divided in their allegiance; in some regions, such as Suffolk, the figure was lower, in others rather higher. Many individual examples can be cited. Oliver Cromwell and much of his immediate family were ardent parliamentarians, but several other members of his family supported the king. The Verney family was deeply divided: while Sir Edmund Verney became the king's standard bearer at Edgehill, and died there, his eldest son and heir supported parliament. When the royalist William Fielding, Earl of Denbigh, was killed in action in spring 1643 he was succeeded by his son, Basil, a parliamentarian. Such divisions probably extended well down the social scale, though surviving sources rarely allow insight into family relations at this level. Although it has occasionally been suggested that families divided in this way as a form of very crude insurance – so that they would have a foot in the victorious camp whoever won – it is most unlikely that this was a serious factor, given the risk of one family member killing another. Wherever letters, diaries, journals and such like survive to explain divided allegiances, it is clear that those allegiances rested on fundamental divisions of faith or principle, on passionately held though divergent beliefs which tore families apart and caused enormous grief and suffering.

The disruption and dislocation of civil war could disturb family life and cause the pain not only of divided allegiance but also of physical separation, of husband and wife, of parent and child. Thus in summer 1643 Lord Henry Spencer, who was besieging Gloucester, was uplifted to receive a letter from his wife, his 'Dearest Heart': 'Just as I was coming out of the trenches ... I received your Letter ... which gave me so much satisfaction that it put all the inconveniences of this Siege out of my thoughts ... writing to you and hearing from you being the most pleasant entertainment that I am capable of in any place; but especially here, where, but

when I am in the trenches (which place is seldom without my company) I am more solitary than I ever was in my life.' Spencer survived the unsuccessful siege operation but was killed a month later at Newbury. In 1644 Susan Rodway wrote to her 'Dear and loving husband, my king love', away serving in the parliamentary operation against Basing House, terribly concerned about the lack of any news from him: 'You do not consider that I am a lone woman, I thought you would never leave me this long together ... So I rest ever praying for your safe return.' It is unlikely that the prayer was answered, for Rodway's unit suffered heavy losses during the unsuccessful operation.

On the other hand, the civil wars also presented greater freedoms. A few elite women were able to play a conspicuous role, which would normally have been denied them in peacetime. Queen Henrietta Maria actively rallied support for her husband at home and abroad, the Countess of Derby held Lathom House for the king, Lady Mary Bankes defended Corfe Castle against parliamentary forces and Lady Brilliana Harley held Brampton Bryan for parliament. But more generally, many women found themselves running households and small businesses while their husbands or fathers were away at war or because their menfolk had perished in the fighting. In some besieged strongholds such as Lyme Regis and Chester, women inhabitants took a semi-military role, putting out fires, reloading muskets, helping to strengthen the earthwork defences. The civil war also brought women greater sexual risks and opportunities. Although a few cases of rape by soldiers were well attested and usually punished severely, rape shows up surprisingly rarely in surviving accounts of the war, even in the propaganda deliberately inflating the ill-discipline and cruelty of enemy troops. With thousands of young men away from home and on the move around the country, there were increased opportunities for consensual sexual encounters. The overall level of illegitimacy does not appear to have risen greatly during the war years, but many parish registers record the inevitable consequence of soldiers quartered and socialising in communities: 'Joan the daughter of a soldier his name unknown but quartered in Edward Phillip's house'. There were many wartime brides, many examples of soldiers in service catching an eye and winning a hand in marriage, and although the overall numbers of marriages in England and Wales fell during the opening years of the civil war, by 1645–46 they had returned to their pre-war average of around 43,000 per year.

While a significant minority of the adult male population took up arms or had them thrust into their hands and fought in the civil wars, a clear majority of the population did not. Again, statistical evidence is available only for the landed elite, whose stance can generally be reconstructed from surviving records. This class would also have been exempt from conscription, so if they did make a clear commitment it would have been through choice. A whole string of local studies, of different parts of England and Wales and encompassing predominantly royalist and parliamentary counties as well as divided regions, have generally revealed that only a minority of the landed elite made such a commitment. In Yorkshire a majority of them, around 65 per cent, did participate in the war, but this has proved to be the exception, not the rule. In Cheshire, for example, the figure falls to around 48 per cent, in Lancashire 38 per cent, and in Suffolk just 14 per cent. Levels of non-elite participation are harder to judge, but the overall figures suggest that through a mixture of voluntary recruiting drives and conscription, a total of up to 150,000 men may have been in arms at the height of the campaigning seasons of 1643, 1644 and 1645, with several thousand more actively involved and participating in the central and local administrative machines of king and parliament. Even at the height of the campaigning seasons, therefore, well over 80 per cent of the adult male population of England and Wales were not actively and directly participating in the war.

Apathy and more organised neutralism were very evident in the opening phase of the war. Many adopted the line of Jonathan Langley of Shropshire, who felt loyalty 'to king and to parliament', who saw good and bad in both parties and nothing but harm in armed conflict between them and who therefore resolved not to take up arms for either side. Although sufficient numbers of elite and non-elite had responded to the initial call to arms to raise armies and wage the Edgehill campaign, the opening months of the war were marked by neutralism of this sort. Individuals, families, communities and whole counties attempted to stay out of the war and keep it at arm's length. For example, in December 1642 the small groups of active, committed royalists and parliamentarians in Cheshire signed a neutrality treaty, by which they agreed to demilitarise the county and keep it out of the war; during the first half of 1643 royalist-dominated Cornwall and parliamentarian-dominated Devon signed a similar truce, thereby apparently taking the whole south-west out of the war; and activists in Staffordshire went even further, raising a third force, a neutral army, which would patrol and protect the county's borders and prevent any royalist or parliamentary troops from entering and fighting there. However, in spring and early summer 1643, as king and parliament stepped up their war efforts and dispatched activists backed by bodies of troops to secure the towns and counties of England and Wales, all these neutrality pacts, truces and treaties – 20 or more of them – collapsed or were overwhelmed and the entire country was carved up and militarised.

Neutralism and anti-war sentiments had by no means been silenced and from time to time thereafter they surfaced once more. For example, in high summer 1643 many local civilians reacted against the brutal and ill-disciplined presence of the king's army in the Severn valley, as it plundered its way through en route to the failed siege of Gloucester. Some locals waged what was in effect a guerrilla war against the king's army, with bodies of armed farmers roaming the countryside, seeking to pick off stragglers, scouts and messengers, and even prepared to ambush whole cavalry units. During 1643 there were anti-war protests in Kent and several Norfolk towns. However, it was in the closing years of the war that mass, organised and armed civilian unrest really became apparent, in the so-called Clubmen movements and risings.

From December 1644 and on through the last full year of the civil war there emerged well-organised groups of local civilians who worked to control, reduce or remove the impact upon the civilian population of the parliamentary and royalist forces, to do away with wartime taxes, garrisons and conditions and to restore the traditional, peacetime forms. Clubmen movements were active in many parts of south and south-west England, the Welsh Marches and south Wales, but were not seen in other areas. Although feeding on a general war-weariness and taken as a sign of increasing exhaustion and desperation, historians have searched in vain for one or more particular causes of the Clubmen risings, for issues or conditions common to all areas of Clubmen risings but unique to them and not found in other areas which did not witness Clubmen movements in the closing phase of the war. Leadership of the Clubmen usually rested with members of the articulate and literate middle classes, perhaps leavened by the occasional clergyman or minor gentleman, but the bulk of Clubmen were drawn from the ranks of the small farmers, the yeomen and husbandmen. While the south Wales 'peaceable army' allegedly numbered

10,000 and the Wiltshire and Dorset Clubmen claimed that they could jointly raise 20,000 if needed, most groups were rather smaller though still numerically significant, perhaps numbering 2–6,000 at their height. Active in different areas at slightly different times, the Clubmen might work with an advancing parliamentary army to try to expel incumbent royalist forces or vice versa, hoping thereby to end the war more quickly, or they might stand as a neutral third force, employing their assortment of weapons, including crude clubs and agricultural implements, to remove and keep out troops from both sides. In many areas they appear to have been genuinely neutral and non-aligned, though some historians have persuasively argued that in parts of the south-west the Clubmen emerged from partisan communities, from areas where popular royalism or parliamentarianism had been evident earlier in the war. Where it suited the advancing parliamentary forces, they were willing to use the Clubmen in 1645 to help clear the countryside of royalists, but more often they brushed the Clubmen aside using whatever force was necessary, determined to press ahead and conclude the war. Important as a sign of increasing disillusionment and anti-war sentiment, as well as of growing civilian exhaustion and desperation as the fighting dragged on, the impact of the Clubmen upon the course and outcome of the war was limited. The civil war was ended not by neutralism, apathy, antipathy or general exhaustion, but by the total and unconditional military victory of the parliamentary armies in 1645–46.

Civilians' stories

William Davenport of Bramhall, Cheshire, was one of thousands of country gentlemen who tried to stay out the war and remain neutral. Unlike most of them, however, Davenport kept a journal or commonplace book, in which he recorded his 'sufferings', a rather self-pitying account showing the difficulties of maintaining a neutral position and the harassment endured from both sides. Davenport was repeatedly visited by parliamentary troops, who controlled that part of Cheshire and who took away his horses and saddles, his arms, including a 'fowlinge peece' and a 'cocking peece', cash, food and other goods. He was also compelled to pay various parliamentary exactions, including the Propositions and assessments, and from time to time was required to give 'quarter and free entertainment' to parliamentary troops billeted on him. But he also suffered at the hands of royalist forces occasionally passing through. In spring 1644 Rupert's troops plundered horses, 60 bushels of oats and £100-worth of linen, 'besides the rifling and pulling in peeces of my house', and Davenport had to quarter a troop of horse overnight. To cap his miseries, in summer 1644 parliament began pursuing Davenport as a delinquent. The case was heard at Stockport and, after evidence from several witnesses, Davenport conceded that he had attended a royalist muster at the start of the war, though he insisted that he had not actively and willingly supported the royalist cause. He was fined £500 and in March 1645 he reluctantly paid up, 'though not as acknowledging myselfe guilty of delinquency, yet thereby to buy my owne peace and rather than suffer myselfe and my estate to fall into the handes of them of whose unjust proceedings I have already had sufficient tryall, refferring my future successe to the protection of the mighty God of heaven who will right me I hope in His good time.'

Randle Holme was a prosperous Chester citizen who was in the city during its lengthy blockade and siege by parliamentary forces. His description of events, written by a civilian with strong royalist sympathies who endured a prolonged siege operation, was subsequently reworked to form of a single, chronological account of the war. Holme gives a good account of how Chester was strengthened early in the war, its stone walls repaired and lined with earth, its gateways closed up or reinforced with ditches and drawbridges and its extra-mural suburbs to the north and east protected 'according to the modern way of fortification ... [by] a trench and mudwall'. In response to a parliamentary attack in summer 1643, the defenders began the process of clearing the surrounding area, pulling down barns, houses, trees and hedges to ensure that 'the rebells could have no shelter on that side'. As Chester came under increasing pressure, early in 1645 the northern suburb outside the city wall was abandoned, and all the buildings there 'razed to the ground for feare of sheltering the enimy'. Worse followed, for in September the parliamentarians successfully stormed the eastern suburb. Garrison and townspeople were now shut up within the circuit of Roman and medieval stone walls, subjected to heavy parliamentary artillery fire 'which did us some little annoyance and hindered our walking in some streets or places of the citty', and which in due course opened up a couple of breaches in the walls themselves. Attempts by parliamentary troops, fortified by a concoction of 'aqua vitae and gunpowder ... given them to drink', to storm breaches in the east and north walls in September and October were repulsed with heavy losses and the breaches were closed with beds, woolpacks and earth. Holme records the stout defence of the city by the

The medieval Phoenix or King Charles' Tower, at the north-east angle of the walled town of Chester. According to tradition, during a visit to the beleaguered city in September 1645 Charles watched from this tower as the remnants of the defeated royalist army he had ordered to relieve the city struggled back to Chester. Thereafter, parliamentary pressure on Chester greatly increased, with an intense bombardment during the autumn and winter, culminating in the surrender of the royalist garrison the following February. (Author's collection)

civilians working alongside the troops, women as well as men: 'By this tyme our women are all on fire, striving through a gallant emulation to outdoe our men and will make good our yielding walls or loose their lives. Seven are shot and three slain, yet they scorn to leave their undertaking.' Holme records the parliamentary change of tactics in November and December, when they began lobbing exploding mortars into the town, 'a wide mouth'd morterpeice in which like the mouth of Etna spits little mountaines in our faces and grinds our dwellings into dust and ashes'. The mortars, generally employed at night to add to the fear and terror, unnerved some of the defenders: 'our women like soe many she astronomers have so glew'd their eyes to heaven in expectation of a second thunder that they canot easily be got to bed lest they dreame of a granado.' Holme's description of the mortar attack on 10 December deserves to be quoted in full, for it gives a wonderful insight into the horrors of civilians under attack:

they are resolved … to conjure heaven and earth to conspire with them for our destruction. Eleaven huge granadoes, like so many tumbling demy-phaetons threaten to set the citty, if not the world on fire. This was a terrible night indeed, our houses like so many splitt vessels crash their supporters and burst themselves in sunder through the very violence of these descending firebrands. The Talbott, an house adjoyning to the Eastgate, flames outright; our hands are busied in quenching this whilst the law of nature bids us leave and seeke our owne security. Being thus distracted anothere Thunder-cracke invites our eyes to the most miserable spectacle that spite could possibly present us with – two houses in the Watergate Streete skippes joynt from joynt and creates an earthquake, the maine posts josell each othere, whilst the frighted casements fly for feare, in a word the whole fabrick is a perfect chaos lively set forth in this metamorphosis. The granmother, mother and three children are struck stark dead and buried in the ruins [of] this

humble edifice, a sepulchre well worth the enimye's remembrance. But for all this they are not satisfied, women and children have not blood enough to quench their fury, and therefore about midnight they shoot seven more in the hope of greater execution, one of these light in an old man's bedchamber, almost dead with age, and send him some few dayes sooner to his grave then perhapps was given him. The next day, six more break in amongst us, one of which persuade an old woman to beare the old man company to heaven, because the times were evill. Our ladyes all this while, like wise merchants, keepe their sellers and will not venture forth in these tymes of danger.

Holme's account breaks off shortly after and his last entry is dated Christmas Day 1645. Roughly five weeks later, the now semi-ruinous city surrendered.

Sir John Oglander was a country gentleman of Nunwell on the Isle of Wight. Although strongly royalist in sympathy, he did not play an active part in the war – he was approaching 60 at its outbreak – and the Isle of Wight itself was firmly but peacefully under parliamentary control throughout. As a royalist living in a parliamentary area, Oglander came under strong suspicion and his commonplace books paints a gloomy picture of his and the island's life during the war. He was arrested several times and held either on the Isle of Wight itself or in London, where he was a prisoner as his wife lay dying at Nunwell in June 1644. The entry in his commonplace book reveals his devastation: 'O my poor wife, with my blood I write it. Thy death hath made me most miserable.' From 1642 he was deprived of all offices, suffered assorted 'affronts and disgraces', was plundered and had to pay over £40 a year in parliamentary taxes. As for the island as a whole, he claimed that 'death, plunder, sales and sequestrations' condemned the elite to 'another world or beggar's bush', that corrupt upstarts such as peddlers, apothecaries, bakers and farmers were put in charge of affairs and were doing 'whatsoever they thought good in their own

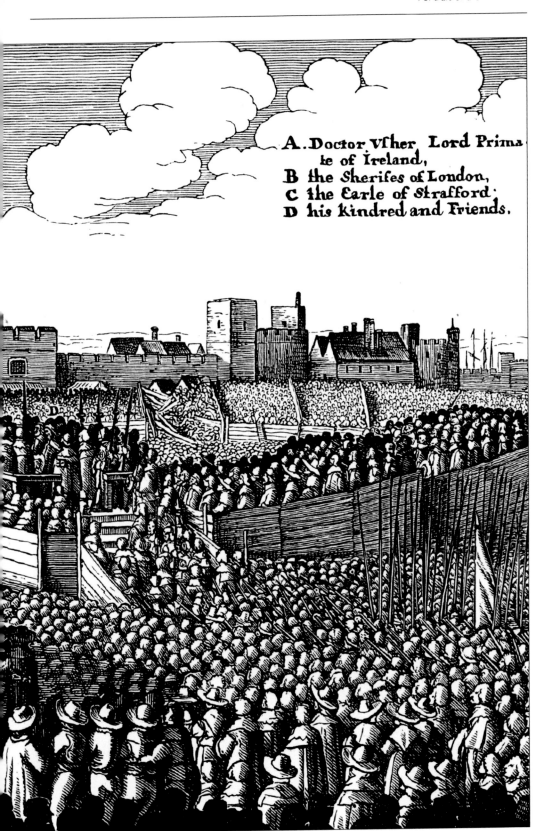

A. Doctor Vsher Lord Prima te of Ireland,
B the Sherifes of London,
C the Earle of Strafford.
D his kindred and Friends.

eyes' and that everywhere had been reduced to a sorry state, 'a melancholy, dejected, sad place – no company, no resort, no neighbours seeing one of the other'.

Nehemiah Wallington was a London wood-turner, in his mid-40s at the outbreak of war. Like Oglander, he played no military part, but unlike him he initially welcomed the war and viewed parliamentary successes as gifts from God. The titles as well as the contents of Wallington's 50 volumes of writings and reflections amply reveal his own puritan faith and parliamentary sympathies: 'A black cover book called The Wonder-Working God, or The God that Worketh Wonders, wherein you may see how the Lord from Fast to Fast answers prayers and giving us many great victories in 1643 and 1644' and 'A black cover book called A Record of Mercies Continued, or Yet God is Good to Israel, shewing how God answers our prayers from Fast to Fast in many victories, 1645'. Wallington despised the religious policy of Charles I, felt intense sympathy for its victims and was amongst those who joyously witnessed Strafford's execution in May 1641. He embraced the destruction of Arminianism, which had been a 'hellish plot to undermine and overturn the gospel', and when the stained glass in London churches was smashed in 1641–42 he kept a fragment 'to show to the generation to come what God hath done for us, to give us such a reformation that our forefathers never saw the like'. Although never apparently tempted to take up arms himself, Wallington supported parliament's fight, sought out newspapers and other pamphlets and guardedly welcomed news of military successes; even the military setbacks of 1643 did not unduly worry him, for he felt that God would rescue His cause. However, though victory might facilitate 'the blessed Reformation both of Church and Commonwealth', by the mid-1640s Wallington was becoming increasingly disillusioned by all the 'pillaging and plundering', the 'most barbarous, bloody, cruel exploits', perpetrated, he was all too aware, by both sides in the civil war.

PREVIOUS PAGE A contemporary illustration of the execution of Sir Thomas Wentworth, Earl of Strafford, on Tower Hill in May 1641. The London wood-turner Nehemiah Wallington was probably amongst the 100,000 Londoners who attended the event and certainly he actively supported the execution of Charles I's right-hand man. Wallington wrote in his journals that the king's reluctance to sign the death warrant 'did strike us all in a damp', he joined in mass protests against Strafford and he described the eventual execution of 'this great Goliath' on 12 May as 'to the joy of the Church of God.' (Ann Ronan Picture Library)

The failure of peace and the renewal of war, 1646–49

The main civil war of 1642–46 ended, not with a huge, decisive battle, but with the conclusion of the parliamentary mopping up operation, as the New Model Army captured the last besieged royalist strongholds and accepted the surrender of the few remaining royalist troops. Although a handful of outposts held out in futile resistance a while longer, in summer 1646 the king himself surrendered and parliament secured complete military victory. Historians ascribe that victory to a number of different factors – parliamentary control of London and the most populous and prosperous parts of the country; the growing financial, material and demographic exhaustion of the less populous and prosperous royalist territories, so making it likely that parliament, not the king, would win a long war; parliamentary control of the navy and therefore of the seas; the advantages that parliament's Scottish alliance brought, especially when compared to the king's divisive and unhelpful dealings with Ireland; the greater skills of individual commanders, the better discipline within the army or the greater efficiency of the military command structure found on parliament's side; the greater efficiency of the wartime political, administrative and fiscal machines that parliament created, compared to those of the king; stronger religious or secular motivation on parliament's side; and key mistakes in the royalist conduct of the war, such as the failure of the king quickly to smash his way into London in autumn 1642 after Edgehill, the abortive and wasteful sieges of Gloucester and Hull in summer 1643 and Rupert's decision to give battle at Marston Moor in summer 1644.

The ending of open hostilities did not lead to a firm peace. The king refused clearly and sincerely to accept any of the various settlements offered to him in 1646–47 and instead sought to divide and rule, hoping that his opponents would fall out amongst themselves and that he would thereby regain regal power, with or without further fighting. He did not have to be particularly perceptive to see the opportunities for this, for even before the war had ended fracture lines were opening up within and between his enemies. The English parliament was divided in a number of ways, but particularly between those on the one hand who favoured a fairly moderate political and constitutional deal with the king in order to restore something approaching the pre-war normality as quickly as possible and who also wanted to reimpose a single state church to which everyone must conform, and on the other hand those who still distrusted Charles and wanted to impose a tight and severe political and constitutional settlement giving the crown very limited power, and who favoured religious freedom for a range of Protestant groups and faiths. There were growing clashes between the former, the Presbyterians, and the latter, the Independents, not only over the future of church and state but also over what to do with the parliamentary army now that war was over. The Presbyterians wished to see most of the army either shipped across to fight in Ireland or quickly disbanded, rightly suspecting that the majority of them supported the political, constitutional and religious policies of the Independents. The Independent political faction, increasingly outvoted in parliament, began looking to military support and pressure as the only chance of attaining its goals.

For its part, the army had purely military grievances it wished to see addressed, including payment of the substantial arrears of pay that had mounted up during the war, full legal indemnity to prevent future

The medieval castle and adjoining walled town of Pembroke had been held for parliament throughout the civil war of 1642–46, and for much of that war had been almost the only parliamentary stronghold in Wales. But in 1648 town and castle became the focus of rebellion against parliamentary rule and during the summer they endured a prolonged siege by Cromwell and part of the New Model Army. (Author's collection)

prosecution for wartime actions, provision for the widows and children of fallen colleagues and acceptance that service in Ireland was to be voluntary. But over and above these demands, during 1646–47 the parliamentary army as a whole, and parts of its rank and file in particular, gave vent to increasingly radical demands for a say in the future political, constitutional and religious settlement of the country. Army radicalism and possible insubordination began to worry some of the senior officers, and cleavages opened up within the parliamentary army as well as between it and the Presbyterian majority in parliament. Lurking in the wings were the Scots, parliament's military allies during the war, who had honoured their part of the 1643 treaty by supplying a large army that had helped win the war. Now the Scots wanted a say in the future settlement of England and Wales and, in particular, they expected parliament to honour its side of the deal by imposing a Scottish-style Presbyterian religious settlement. Many in parliament and much of the army bitterly opposed the re-imposition of any single state church, viewing the wartime collapse of the Church of England and the fragmentation of Protestant beliefs as a gift from God to be cherished and preserved.

The situation in England and Wales remained tense. A whole range of radical political, religious, social and economic ideas had been unleashed by the war, fostered and spread in printed works that had proliferated since the effective collapse of state censorship in 1641. Taking advantage of the *de facto* religious toleration of the war years, new Protestant sects had sprung up in England and Wales, including Independents, Presbyterians and Baptists. Groups pressing for extensive changes to the constitution and the social and economic order, most notably the Levellers, had gained strong support in parts of England and Wales, both in the army and amongst the civilian population. In the absence of a firm settlement with the king, church and state remained in flux, the future uncertain, and wartime conditions dragged on, even though the war itself had

ended. Thus in 1646–47 there was no swift return to traditional peacetime forms. Instead local government remained in the hands of military-backed county committees, the strong military presence in garrisons and army camps continued, there appeared to be no end to the fragmented religious situation and, above all perhaps, the very heavy and repeated wartime taxes continued unabated. All this came on top of the material and financial exhaustion of the war years themselves, very apparent in many areas by 1645–46. The king saw and seized an opportunity to capitalise on this discontent and on the divisions amongst his opponents by making a bid to reassert royal power. Even though he was a prisoner of the parliamentary army, in the winter of 1647–48 he concluded a treaty with the Scots, promising to impose Scottish Presbyterianism in England and Wales for an experimental period in return for military aid, and he began encouraging his supporters south of the border to rise up in his favour.

Between spring and autumn 1648 there were riots, risings and rebellions in many parts of England and Wales, some of them well-planned and well-organised, others apparently spontaneous responses to local circumstances. Some seem to have originated as vigorous protests against the continuing presence of troops and garrisons, county committees and heavy taxes, while others, particularly in southern and eastern England, were from the outset pro-royalist in nature, organised and led by overt and committed supporters of the king seeking to restore Charles to power. Elsewhere, particularly in south and south-west Wales, the lead was taken by disillusioned former parliamentarians. Lack of pay and discontent with its leaders also prompted a mutiny in the parliamentary navy in summer 1648. Most of the disturbances, including those in Cornwall, Surrey, Norfolk, Lincolnshire, Yorkshire and North Wales, either fizzled out of their own accord or were easily contained and crushed by local parliamentary forces. But in two regions the threat was more serious and was dealt with by the New Model Army. In May Sir Thomas Fairfax led 7,000 New Model troops to crush a royalist rising in Kent. Having secured several towns and castles, on the evening of 1 June Fairfax led his main force into the rebel stronghold of Maidstone and took the town after a night battle. However, many of the rebels got away and managed to cross the Thames estuary into Essex, where they rendezvoused with further rebel forces. With Fairfax in pursuit, they holed up in Colchester and strongly fortified the town. There followed a long and bitter formal siege from 12 June until late August, when Colchester was eventually starved into submission. Oliver Cromwell, meanwhile, had led up to 8,000 New Model troops west in early May to crush the rebellion in south Wales. In fact, the rebel field army was defeated by local forces at St Fagans on 8 May, before their arrival, and, having mopped up Chepstow and Tenby, Cromwell's main objective in south Wales became the capture of the rebel-held town and castle of Pembroke. This he besieged from 24 May until its surrender on 11 July. Almost immediately Cromwell marched north to engage a Scottish-royalist army which had eventually begun rolling south. Resistance in Scotland to the treaty with the king had delayed the raising of forces, and not until early July had a Scottish army of around 10,000 men crossed the border, following the west coast route via Carlisle. Poorly led, poorly supplied and picking up very little support in northern England, the army made steady but rather slow progress south. Marching north at speed, Cromwell first crossed into Yorkshire to pick up reinforcements and then swung west, crossing the Pennines to fall in behind the Scottish-royalist army. Although leaving open the road to London, Cromwell's manoeuvre severed his opponent's line of retreat back to Scotland. The battle of

Preston of 17 August was, in reality, merely the first stage of a running battle that continued through Wigan and Winwick to Warrington over the following days, as Cromwell picked off and destroyed the various elements of the disorganised and disjointed Scottish army.

The second civil war, as this series of home-grown rebellions and Scottish-royalist invasion are sometimes called, was particularly brutal and bitter. It was fought in dreadful weather, perhaps the wettest summer of the century, and it came to focus on two intense, protracted and unpleasant sieges. The parliamentary army resented the revived threat to peace and held their opponents personally responsible for the renewed fighting and bloodshed. As they secured military victory, they were determined to exact revenge and justice on the perpetrators. Ordinary prisoners were harshly treated, held for prolonged periods in unsavoury conditions, and parliament laid plans to send many of them, English, Welsh and Scots, to work in Barbados. The officers were treated even more harshly. The two royalist leaders captured at Colchester, Sir Charles Lucas and Sir George Lisle, were promptly condemned and shot. The three leaders of the Welsh rebellion were likewise condemned, but eventually only one of them, John Poyer, chosen by lot, was executed by firing squad in London. In December the army purged parliament of its opponents and of the moderate members who, even as the second civil war was being waged, had continued to show a willingness to conclude a deal with Charles. This left a 'Rump' of pro-army, anti-Charles hard men who, with the army's continuing support, set up a high court to try and execute the king in January 1649. Several other royalists who had played a prominent role in 1648, including Lords Capel, Holland and Hamilton, soon followed him to the block.

The legacy of the civil wars

There were profound changes and innovations in England and Wales during the late 1640s and the 1650s. The king was tried and executed, the monarchy and the House of Lords were abolished, a republic or commonwealth was established, a succession of regimes and constitutional forms came and went, and, in the absence of a state church, Protestant plurality and a range of other secular and religious ideas flourished. Church and crown lands were sold off and a militarised England and Wales swept on first to establish control over Ireland and Scotland and then to embark on expansionist and quite successful foreign, commercial and colonial policies. None of this was the inevitable consequence of the

civil wars, but it is hard to image that most or all of these developments would have come about without the searing experience of civil war in England and Wales.

The civil wars left a trail of mutilated bodies in their wake. Like Richard Gough's neighbour, whose leg had been smashed by a musket ball and who was 'very crooked as

The rather fragmentary ruins of the 13th-century, hill-top castle above Montgomery, looking north across the middle ward towards the inner ward. Like scores of castles in England and Wales, in summer 1649 parliament ordered Montgomery castle to be slighted to render it indefensible. A team of workmen removed the valuable and reusable materials, including timber, tiles and glass, before most of the masonry walls were brought down. (Author's collection)

long as he lived', William Blundell struggled on in pain for the best part of half a century after his leg had been badly broken in action in March 1643. Once 'a pretty straight young thing, all dashing in scarlet' in his captain's uniform, by the 1650s he was portraying himself rather differently: 'But now, if you chance to hear a thing come – Thump – Thump – up your stairs like a knocker, God bless us, at midnight, look out confidently: a gross full body … The thing is no goblin, but the very party that we talk on.' In 1649 Thomas Oulton recalled that six years earlier he had been shot through his left leg while pursuing Capel's royalists out of Cheshire, 'by which shotte hee is mayhemed and shall bee lame whilest hee liveth', though he had evidently returned to military service later in the war, only to be wounded in action at Chester where he 'lost very much of his blood', making him 'disinabled in his body to worke for his liveinge'. At the end of the war Thomas Hinchcliffe of Kettleshulme in the foothills of the Pennines had received a dozen wounds in the battle of Worcester, having 'his left eare wholly cutt away from his head and soe utterly lost' and also 'the elbowe of his left Arme cut away'. Such examples proliferate in the surviving records of local government, as the maimed and the damaged relayed their tales of woe in search of a pension or other financial handout. During the 1650s these petitioners stressed service in the parliamentary army, while after the Restoration they naturally claimed to have received wounds fighting valiantly for the late king.

The civil war left other physical scars on the landscape of England and Wales. Many towns had been reduced to a semi-ruinous condition by the end, a consequence of the deliberate demolition of outer suburbs, of the effects of bombardment by cannon and mortar and of the fires that swept through several towns in the course of defensive or offensive operations. Such urban damage was generally repaired within a generation or two and even the most devastated towns – Bridgwater, Bristol, Chester and Colchester – recovered in time. Most churches damaged

in the course of the fighting were also restored and repaired, though a handful had to be completely rebuilt. On the other hand, the civil wars often marked the end of the effective lifespan of most masonry castles. Although few castles re-fortified and garrisoned during the war had been completely wrecked by the military operations mounted against them and many had stood up remarkably well to bombardment and attack from 17th-century artillery and armies, in the wake of the war parliament took a deliberate political decision to render castles untenable and so prevent their re-use in any renewed civil war. In the late 1640s and early 1650s scores of castles in England and Wales were slighted in this way, their walls and gatehouses extensively or selectively brought down so that they could play no further military role. Buildings that had dominated many towns and much of the countryside of England and Wales since the time of the Normans came crashing down. Within a couple of generations they were seen as items of aesthetic and antiquarian interest, romantic and ivy-clad ruins, embellishments to the parks and estates of the refined Georgian era.

The efficient military and fiscal machines created by parliament during the 1640s to wage and win the civil wars were soon put to wider use. The victory in England and Wales in 1648 led not to a period of peace but to a change in the nature and location of the fighting. The English state was determined to restore its power and control over Ireland and by 1649 it had both the means and the opportunity to do so. In 1649–50 Oliver Cromwell led a large part of the New Model Army in an often brutal but highly effective military campaign in Ireland that broke the back of Irish Catholic resistance. He was succeeded by other commanders who completed the process of reconquest and then by semi-military, semi-civilian governors who ran Ireland in the Protestant interest, dispossessing and displacing much of the Irish Catholic population and enforcing greater union with, but also very much under, England. Cromwell had left Ireland in spring 1650 in order to lead a campaign against the Scots, who were giving wary support to the late king's son and who appeared thereby to be threatening the English republic. In 1650–51 Cromwell campaigned in Scotland against a canny enemy that generally refused to give battle in the open. Frustrated by the Scottish leaders' propensity to fall back into the highlands and determined not to suffer a second winter in Scotland, in late summer 1651 Cromwell deliberately threatened the Scottish army from the north-east while leaving the lowlands and the road south temptingly unguarded. The Scots took the bait and headed into England. The Scottish-royalist invasion of 1651 was as futile as that of 1648 and attracted as little support south of the border, though it did progress further along the west coast route, getting as far as Worcester by August. There, hemmed in on all sides and greatly outnumbered, the Scottish army and the royalist cause were overwhelmed and destroyed in battle on 3 September, the last major fighting of the civil wars in England and Wales and a battle seen by many historians as ending the sequence of military events that had begun close by at Powick Bridge back in September 1642.

The various non-monarchical, ostensibly civilian regimes that held power during the 1650s were all initially supported by the army, though in due course most fell from favour and were removed by it. There was a strong military presence in both Ireland and Scotland, to guarantee order and English political control, as well as in England and Wales, to ensure that royalists and other opponents were kept at bay. With the principal Irish and Scottish resistance crushed, military resources were deployed abroad, initially in a rather low-key and indecisive naval war against the Dutch, but then in a much more active and successful naval, colonial and Continental war against Catholic Spain. The continuing military presence and expansive foreign policy gave the regimes strength at home and respect abroad, but also brought increasing financial strain, in spite of the high level of taxation maintained throughout the 1650s. Despite occasional flurries of persecution, with army pressure and support the regimes also maintained the broad liberty of conscience seen during the war years, with no single state church and with effective toleration for just about all the Protestant sects and faiths that had sprung up since the wars began.

In many ways the Restoration of 1660, with the unconditional return of the Stuarts and of traditional, hereditary monarchy in the person of Charles I's eldest son, Charles II, seemed to mark the reversal of many of the achievements and much of the immediate legacy of the civil wars. Traditional government via a powerful king with an extensive prerogative who chose to call occasional parliaments returned; the enforced British union of the 1650s was undone and Scotland and Ireland regained their own parliaments; much of the army was disbanded, peace was made abroad and the normal 17th-century foreign policy of complex diplomacy but a profound unwillingness to commit resources to war, especially a land war, resurfaced. Although many of the pre-war sources of income were not restored in 1660, Charles II's finances reverted to semi-traditional forms, and taxes were reduced; the Church of England was restored as the only available faith and everyone was compelled to belong and adhere to the Anglican church; and crown and church recovered most of their pre-war estates.

On the other hand, many of the changes that had emerged during or in the wake of the English civil wars were not completely undone or forgotten. Historians often talk rather airily about seeds sown during the civil wars and the 1650s, which then lay covered and dormant during the Restoration era but burst back into life the Glorious Revolution of 1688, which removed Charles II's brother, James II, from the throne and replaced him with a different monarchy, that of William III and Mary II, and a different form and style of government. By the 1690s parliament had attained a much stronger and more secure position in central

Charles II, by or after Samuel Cooper. His Restoration in 1660 in some ways reversed the achievements of the civil wars, though in other ways an enduring legacy survived to influence and shape England and Britain in the later 17th century and beyond. (Ann Ronan Picture Library)

government and administration; a further fiscal revolution revived some of the innovations of the civil war period and enabled huge sums to be found to finance renewed expansion of the armed forces; England again began playing an active and outgoing role overseas, with war by land and sea and ambitious foreign, colonial and commercial policies supported by military might. In the wake of the Protestant plurality of the mid-17th century, the religious monopoly supposedly regained by

OPPOSITE AND ABOVE Some of the officers and men who defended Chester for the king during the civil war, as depicted in a memorial window, erected in Farndon church, Cheshire, after the Restoration. These photographs show not the window itself, but rather parts of a nineteenth century painting of the glass, commissioned by a Victorian Dean of Chester who rescued and restored the window. (Author's collection)

the Church of England at the Restoration had proved divisive and unrealistic and by the 1690s most Protestant groups and faiths outside the Anglican church had gained official, legal toleration. Finally, in the opening decade of the 18th century, Scotland and England reunited as a single political unit, though reunification with Ireland would not come for another century.

It is not always clear how far these late 17th-century developments can be linked to the mid-century innovations, and to what degree a line of continuum can be traced in political, constitutional, military, fiscal, foreign and religious affairs between the consequences of the civil wars of the 1640s and the consequences of the Glorious Revolution. In religion, the link is clear, for the Protestant plurality created in the 1640s and 1650s could never be reversed, despite the Restoration settlement, and this led finally to the Toleration Act of 1689. In other areas, however, the links are far less clear and tangible.

As he sat writing his history of Myddle in old age, Richard Gough pulled together his memories of the civil wars of his boyhood and of the involvement of his neighbours in the conflict. Several had been sequestrated or plundered, one moving away to escape his tormentors, another suffering so much that 'he took an extreme grief and died'. One neighbour had gone off to fight for the king, as much to escape his debts as out of principle, had served throughout the war and had eventually returned bringing 'nothing home but a crazy body and many scars, the symptoms of the dangerous service which he had performed'. Another neighbour had served during the war as a messenger for the parliamentary garrison at Wem, deliberately going about dressed in ragged clothes to pass as a beggar, carrying papers in a hollowed-out stick; if he encountered enemy soldiers en route he would 'throw his stick at birds, so that it might go over the hedge, and then go over to fetch it' once the soldiers had passed. The pro-royalist rector of Myddle had been ejected by parliament after the war, though as an absentee who had allowed church property in Myddle to fall ruinous, Gough had little sympathy for him. The civil war had touched Richard Gough and his generation, had been a formative experience

and one they never forgot, and stories about the conflict repeatedly weave in and out of Gough's much broader account. But life had continued and the world had moved on. Gough told the story of one William Preece, also known as 'Scoggan', a veteran of the Thirty Years' War, who had enlisted for the king at Shrewsbury in late summer 1642. He had fought in Shropshire throughout the war and at one stage was captured and held prisoner at Wem but soon escaped. On another occasion, as governor of a minor royalist garrison, he saw off a parliamentary attack with a mixture of bluff, shouting orders to large numbers of men under his command when in reality 'he had but eight in all', and open violence, taking a pot shot with his fowling piece at one of his enemies whom he recognised as a local tailor. During the war he had married for a second time, but his wife soon died. 'This Scoggan, after the wars, came to Whixall, and there married a third wife. He was not troubled by the parliament party, as many others were; for he that sits on the ground can fall no lower. So he died in peace.'

Further reading

The best general history of the 17th century as a whole is probably B. Coward, *The Stuart Age* (1994), though D. Hirst, *England in Conflict 1603–1660* (1999) is also excellent on the decades down to the Restoration. The period 1625–60 is explored in detail by A. Woolrych, *Britain in Revolution* (2002).

The reign of James VI and I is best approached through R. Lockyer, *James VI and I* (1998), P. Croft, *James I* (2002), C. Durston, *James I* (1993) and S. J. Houston, *James I* (1995), and the reign of Charles I through M. Young, *Charles I* (1997), B. Quintrell, *Charles I, 1625–40* (1993) and C. Durston, *Charles I* (1998).

The debate on the causes of the English civil wars is surveyed by R. C. Richardson, *The Debate on the English Revolution Revisited* (1998), and the whole field is analysed by A. Hughes, *The Causes of the English Civil War* (1998) and N. Carlin, *The Causes of the English Civil War* (1998).

C. Russell takes a generally top-down view of the long-, medium- and short-term causes of the war in *The Causes of the English Civil War* (1990) and *The Fall of the British Monarchies, 1637–42* (1991), while A. Fletcher's *The Outbreak of the English Civil War* (1981) focuses on the contribution of provincial opinion and attitudes.

There are many, mainly military histories of the civil wars. Amongst the best or the most recent general histories are P. Young and R. Holmes, *The English Civil War* (1974), R. Ollard, *This War Without an Enemy* (1976), A. Woolrych, *Battles of the English Civil War* (1992), J. Adair, *By the Sword Divided* (1997), M. Bennett, *The Civil Wars in Britain and Ireland* (1997), S. Reid, *All the King's Armies* (1998), J. P. Kenyon and J. Ohlmeyer (eds), *The Civil Wars* (1998) and J. S. Wheeler, *The Irish and British Wars* (2002).

More specialist, technical aspects of the war are explored by D. Blackmore, *Arms and Armour of the English Civil War* (1990), K. Roberts, *Soldiers of the English Civil War I. Infantry* (1989) and J. Tincey, *Soldiers of the English Civil War II. Cavalry* (1990).

J. Barratt, *Cavaliers* (2000) explores the war from a royalist perspective, and I. Gentles, *The New Model Army* (1992) examines the role of the principal parliamentary army in war and politics 1645–53; see also M. Kishlansky, *The Rise of the New Model Army* (1997). C. Carlton, *Going to the Wars* (1992) is a superb examination of the mainly military experience of fighting, while M. Bennett, *The Civil Wars Experienced* (2000) looks at the British wars through civilian eyes.

Much of the best recent work on the civil wars has taken a regional or local perspective, some of it focusing on the local elites, some of it attempting to reconstruct popular opinion and 'the people's war'. J. Morrill's *Revolt of the Provinces* (1980), reissued as *Revolt in the Provinces* (1998) shows how the provinces of England and Wales related and reacted to events at the centre 1630–50.

Among the best studies of particular regions are D. Underdown, *Revel, Riot and Rebellion* (1985) on the south-west, J. Wroughton, *Unhappy Civil War* (1999) also on the south-west, P. Tennant, *Edgehill and Beyond* (1992) on the South Midlands, C. Holmes, *The Eastern Association* (1974), R. Sherwood, *Civil War in the Midlands* (1992) and R. Hutton, *The Royalist War Effort* (1999) on the royalists at war in Wales and the Marches. P. Gaunt, *A Nation Under Siege* (1991) also explores the civil war in Wales.

Among the best county studies are A. Hughes, *Politics, Society and the Civil War in Warwickshire* (1987), J. Morrill, *Cheshire 1630–60* (1974), M. Stoyle, *Loyalty and Locality: Popular Allegiances in Devon* (1994), A.

Duffin, *Faction and Faith: The Political Allegiances of the Cornish Gentry* (1996), M. Wolffe, *Gentry Leaders in Peace and War* (1997) on Devon, M. Atkin, *The Civil War in Worcestershire* (1995) and K. Parker, *Radnorshire from Civil War to Restoration* (2000).

Among the best town studies are D. Underdown, *Fire from Heaven* (1992) on Dorchester, M. Stoyle, *From Deliverance to Destruction* (1996) on Exeter, J. Lynch, *For King and Parliament* (1998) on Bristol, M. Atkin and L. Laughlin, *Gloucester and the Civil War* (1992), P. Tennant, *The Civil War in Stratford upon Avon* (1996) and S. Porter, *London and the Civil War* (1996).

J. Morrill has edited two excellent collections on various aspects of the impact of the civil wars – *Reactions to the English Civil War* (1982) and *The Impact of the English Civil War* (1991). The fullest assessment of the physical destruction is S. Porter, *Destruction in the English Civil War* (1994),

while the physical remains of the war are explored in P. Gaunt, *The Cromwellian Gazetteer* (1986) and P. Harrington, *Archaeology of the English Civil War* (1992).

R. Ashton, *Counter Revolution: The Second Civil War and its Origins* (1994) is a detailed study of the years 1646–48 and A. Woolrych, *Soldiers and Statesmen* (1987) is a masterly account of the parliamentary army and army politics in 1647. D. Underdown, *Pride's Purge* (1971) is a detailed analysis of the army and of political developments in the wake of the second civil war.

The military campaign in Ireland of 1649–50 is assessed in very different ways by J. S. Wheeler, *Cromwell in Ireland* (1999) and T. Reilly, *Cromwell, An Honourable Enemy* (1999). J. Grainger, *Cromwell Against the Scots* (1997) recounts the Scottish campaign of 1650–51, while M. Atkin, *Cromwell's Crowning Mercy* (1998) explores the campaign and battle of Worcester.

Index

Figures in **bold** refer to illustrations